The Complete Book
of Toasts

Other Books by Paul Dickson

Think Tanks

The Great American Ice Cream Book

The Future of the Workplace

The Electronic Battlefield

The Mature Person's Guide to Kites, Yo-Yos, Frisbees, and Other Childlike Diversions

Out of This World

The Future File

Chow: A Cook's Tour of Military Food

The Official Rules

The Official Explanations

Words

There Are Alligators in the Sewers & Other American Credos (with Joseph C. Goulden)

Jokes

Names

On Our Own: A Declaration of Independence for the Self-Employed

The Library in America

Family Words

The Dickson Baseball Dictionary

The New Official Rules

What Do You Call a Person From . . . ?

Slang!

Timelines

Baseball's Greatest Quotations

The Complete Book
of Toasts

Paul Dickson

ROBSON BOOKS

This paperback edition published in Great Britain in 2004 by Robson Books,
The Chrysalis Building, Bramley Road, London, W10 6SP

An imprint of Chrysalis Books Group plc

British Library Cataloguing in Publication Data
A catalogue record for this title is available from the British Library.

ISBN 1 86105 803 9

Printed by Creative Print & Design (Wales), Ebbw Vale

Here's
to the
Toast

. . . and to the reader in the form of a toast from Edith Lea Chase and W. E. P. French's genre classic of 1903, *Toasts for All Occasions:*

> A health, O reader, and 'tis our adieu:
> Good luck, good health, good fortune wait on you.
> Over the wine please note our loving look:—
> *Waes Hael! Hoch! Skoal! Prosit! Buy the book.*

Contents

Introduction 1

A Brief History of
Raised Glasses 6

How to Use This
Book 27

Toasts and Toasting . . 28

Age 28

Alliterative 32

Anniversaries 34

Babies & Children . . . 36

Beer & Ale 38

Better Times 40

Biblical 42

Birthdays 44

Bulls 46

Celia's Toast (with
variations) 47

Champagne 48

Cheeses 50

Christmas 50

Curses 55

Death 59

England 62

"Excuses for the
Glass" 67

Fishing 69

Food 72

Friendship 75

Contents

General 81

Graces 88

Guests 92

Health 94

Hell & Damnation . . . 95

**Hints for Effective
Toasting** **97**

Historic 99

Home 108

Hosts & Hostesses . . . 109

Husbands 111

International 112

Irish 113

Jewish 120

Latin 121

Libations 121

Limericks 130

Love 131

Luck 138

Lust 140

Man & Men 142

Military 145

Mornings After 148

New Year's 150

Odd Customs **155**

Old Things 157

Parents 157

Parting 158

Past, Present, &
Future 160

Professional &
Occupational 161

Quotes (*which are not
exactly toasts but which
belong in a book like
this*) **172**

Reunions 175

Revelry 176

St. Patrick's Day 181

Scotch 182

Secrets **184**

**A Selected Toast and
Tipple Glossary** **189**

Self & Selves 192

Contents

*   *   *

Shakespearean 194

Skoaling **196**

Special Occasions . . . 197

Special People 203

Spirits (ardent) 208

Sports & Games 211

Temperament 213

Toastmaster 215

Tongue Twisters 216

Ultimate Toasts **217**

Weddings 218

Wine 223

Wives 228

Woman & Women . . 229

World's Worst
Toasts 232

Acknowledgments . . **235**

Bibliography **237**

*   *   *

Toasts

Introduction

"Next to the originator of a good sentence is the first quoter of it."

—RALPH WALDO EMERSON

There are a number of old things which we are well rid of—child labor, the Berlin Wall, scurvy, glass shampoo bottles, and too many others to mention—but there are still others that we are foolish to let slip away. Toasting is one of them.

A toast is a basic form of human expression that can be used for virtually any emotion from love to rage (although raging toasts tend to cross the line into the realm of curses). They can be sentimental, cynical, lyric, comic, defiant, long, short, or even just a single word.

The names and traditions associated with the custom are many and date back to the ancient world. They are also very much a part of our literary heritage and, with the exception of the last few decades, there has not been a writer of note from Milton to Mencken who has not left us at least one good toast. What's more, some of our favorite fictional characters have uttered classics—among them, Tiny Tim's "God bless us every one!" from *A Christmas Carol* and Rick's "Here's lookin' at you, kid!" to Ilse from the 1942 Warner Brothers classic *Casablanca*.

Most important, however, is that they are so useful. They are a medium through which such deep feelings as love, hope, high spirits, and admiration can be quickly, conveniently, and sincerely expressed.

There was a time, not that long ago, when one could not go to a luncheon—let alone a banquet or wedding—without hearing a series of carefully proposed and executed toasts. Toasts were the test of one's ability to come up with an appropriate inspiration to sip to the honor of some person, sentiment, or institution. It really didn't matter if it was an original written for the occasion or a time-tested classic passed down from Elizabethan times. What was important was whether or not the toast worked to keep the proceedings moving at a jolly pace.

About a third of the way into this century, however, the custom of creative, thoughtful toasting began to erode. It seemed as if people had less time and inclination to work them up or memorize them. British author John Pudney wrote in 1963 of "decline in the eloquence and variety of the toast in the English language. The last two generations at least seem to find themselves embarrassed by the formality of toasting."

In recent years, the decline has continued to the point at which a set of wedding toasts may have no more style, grace, or imagination than a clearing of the throat and a hastily yelped, "Here's to the bride and groom! Here's to Fred and Maxine!" Moreover, most of our workaday toasts still in use are of the quick, down-the-hatch variety in which the custom has been reduced to a mumbled word (Cheers!; Prosit!) or phrase (Happy days!; Down the hatch!; Hair on your chest!) uttered from habit rather than any real sentiment.

Ironically, some of the better old toasts have devolved to the level where they are virtually meaningless either because they have been shortened or lost their original context. The ubiquitous "Here's mud in your eye!" is a good case in point. A fuller, much older version ends the line with ". . . while I look over your lovely sweetheart!" "Mud in your eye" had an entirely different context in the days when the American West was opening up. A pioneering farmer about to leave the East would stop in the local tavern to say good-bye to friends, who would toast mud in his eyes. In this situation those proposing the toast were hoping the farmer would find soft, rich, and damp soil that would be thrown up as specks of mud as the farmer ploughed it.

Toasting is still an important custom on such high and formal occasions as state dinners and diplomatic receptions. Yet in this realm, a different kind of erosion has taken place. Official toasts—which have always tended to be light, friendly, and anecdotal—have become political vehicles in recent years. Increasingly, they are long, windy, political addresses.

Things really began to sour in 1975 when Zambian President Kenneth Kaunda startled the guests at a White House dinner when he responded to a traditional toast from President Gerald Ford with a twenty-minute "toast," which in reality was a statement of his nation's foreign policy.

For his part, Ford tried during his White House term but was not beyond the occasional gaff. This was his toast to Anwar Sadat in December 1975: "[To] the great people and the government of Israel—Egypt, excuse me." Ford should not be singled out because in December 1982 President Ronald Reagan rose at a dinner hosted in his honor by the president of Brazil and proposed a toast to "the people of Bolivia."

Enough. The point is often made that we have come close to abandoning a useful medium and form of communication in an age of media and communication. Simply stated, the purpose of this book is to help as a vehicle for a revival. In truth, there have been some bright omens and developments in recent years that signal a new interest in the toast.

So, here's to it! And to fuel and give this revival an extra boost, the following pages contain more than fifteen hundred of the best, most useful, and most literate toasts that could be found. With the help of dozens of people—reference librarians,

museum curators, brewers, distillers, vintners, and old friends—
I have been able to collect something on the order of six thousand different toasts from which the examples in this book were culled.

A Brief History of Raised Glasses

The custom of drinking a "health" to the prosperity, happiness, luck, or good health of another dates back into antiquity—and, perhaps, into prehistory.

It is impossible to point to the moment when the first crude vessel was raised in honor of an ancient god or to the health of a newborn baby. Nor do we have any idea when a parched traveler lifted his cup in thanks to the man or woman who gave him wine.

What we do know is that the custom of drinking to health permeated the ancient world. Ulysses drank to the health of Achilles in the *Odyssey*. An early Greek custom called for a pledge of three cups—one to Mercury, one to the Graces, and one to Zeus. In Rome, drinking to another's health became so important, the Senate decreed that all diners must drink to Augustus at every meal. Fabius Maximus declared that no man should eat or drink before he had prayed for him and drank to his health.

The ancient Hebrews, Persians, and Egyptians were toasters, as were the Saxons, Huns, and other tribes. In *The Decline and Fall of the Roman Empire*, Edward Gibbon tells of a feast among the Huns at which their leader Attila led no less than three rounds of toasts for each course during a dinner of many courses.

Over time the simple act of toasting became embellished and intertwined with other customs. (It would not be until the seventeenth century that the act was actually referred to as a toast. More on that shortly.) At some point along the way, for instance, the gesture of clinking glasses or cups became popular. It has long been believed that this began during the Christian era, as the original intention of the clink was to produce a bell-like noise so as to banish the devil, who is repelled by bells. Another legendary explanation for glass clinking is that all five senses should come into play to get the greatest pleasure from a drink. It is tasted, touched, seen, smelled, and—with the clink—heard.

An odd but essential custom was added to British tippling during the invasion by the Danes during the tenth century. This was the custom of pledging another's health in the most literal terms—that is, a friend stating the intention of guarding a drinker from harm while he tosses back a drink. This stemmed from the objectionable Danish habit of cutting the throats of Englishmen while they were drinking. Shakespeare's line from *Timon of Athens,* "Great men should drink with harness on their throats," is one of several old literary references to this murderous behavior.

Still another morbidly fascinating custom from northern Europe is that of drinking mead or ale from the skull of a fallen enemy. The Scots and Scandinavians both practiced this primitive form of recycling, and the Highland Scotch *skiel* (tub) and the Norse *skoal* (bowl) derive from it. The modern toast, *skoal,* in turn comes from the Old Norse term. This custom persisted through the eleventh century, after which only an occasional skull was converted into a drinking vessel. Lord Byron acquired a human skull, had it mounted as a drinking vessel, and wrote an inscription for it that read:

Toasts

Start not, nor deem my spirit fled:
In me behold the only skull
From which, unlike a living head,
Whatever flows is never dull.

I lived, I loved, I quaff'd like thee:
I died: let earth my bones resign:
Fill up—thou canst not injure me,
The worm hath fouler lips than thine.

Better to hold the sparkling grape,
Than nurse the earthworm's slimy brood;
And circle in the goblet's shape
The drink of gods, than reptile's food.

Where once my wit, perchance, hath shone,
In aid of others let me shine;
And when, alas! our brains are gone,
What nobler substitute than wine?

Quaff while thou canst, another race
When thou and thine, like me, are sped,
May rescue thee from earth's embrace,
And rhyme and revel with the dead.

The first *recorded* instance of a toast being offered in England occurred in A.D. 450 at a great feast given by the British King Vortigern to his Saxon allies. Rowena, the beautiful daughter of the Saxon leader Hengist, held up a large goblet filled with a spiced drink and drank to the king, saying, *"Louerd King, waes hael!"*—"Lord King, be of health!"—to which he replied, *"Drink, hael."*

According to the account of medieval historian Geoffrey of Monmouth, the festivity did not stop there. Vortigern kissed Rowena and then made passionate love to her. Intoxicated, he then bargained with Hengist for her hand. A deal was struck by which Hengist got the province of Kent in exchange for Rowena. Vortigern and Rowena were married that evening.

For at least a thousand years drinking in Britain was commonly accompanied by the same verbal exchange, although *waes hael* became *wassail*. One of the earliest known Christmas carols, dating from the days of the Norman minstrels, ends with these lines:

> Each must drain his cup of wine,
> And I the first will toss off mine:
> Thus I advise,
> Here then I bid you all *Wassail*,
> Cursed be he who will not say *Drink hail*.

Over the years the term wassail became associated with Christmas and the New Year, the times of the greatest festivity, and by the seventeenth century the meaning had narrowed to the specific one of drinking from a large bowl or loving cup on Christmas Day and Twelfth Night. While people of means prepared their own wassail, groups of poor people commonly went from door to door with an empty bowl which they expected to be filled at every stop. Some prefaced their request with a medley of Christmas carols while others chanted something more threatening:

> Come, butler, come fill us a bowl of the best;
> Then we hope that your soul in heaven may rest;
> But if you draw us a bowl of the small,
> Then down shall go butler, bowl and all.

A variation of this custom was for a group to go door to door with a beverage of their own making for which they would expect to be dearly paid. There were songs for this as well:

Toasts

~~~
. . .
~~~

Good dame, here at your door
Our wassail we begin,
We are all maidens poor,
We now pray let us in,
With our wassail.

Some of the old wassailing songs were little more than toasts set to music:

Here's to _____ and his right ear,
God send our maister a Happy New Year;
A Happy New Year as e'er he did see—
With my wassailing bowl I drink to thee.

Here's to _____ and her right eye,
God send our mistress a good Christmas pie:
A good Christmas pie as e'er I did see—
With my wassailing bowl I drink to thee.

The present custom of caroling from door to door derives from all of this.

Although people had been drinking to one another for centuries, the actual term "toast" did not come along until the late seventeenth century, when it was the custom to place a piece of toast or crouton in a drink. This is alluded to in many drinking songs and ditties of the period including this one published in 1684:

A toast is like a sot; or what is most
Compatitive, a sot is like a toast;
For when their substance is liquor sink,
Both properly are said to be in drink.

The exact reason for doing this has been blurred by time, but various hints point to the conclusion that it was either be-

~~~
. . .
~~~

lieved to improve the flavor of the drink in the manner of a spice, or that it was a built-in snack, a bit of token nourishment. Whatever the reason, the practice was common, and virtually anything found floating in a drink was referred to as "toast."

The name change occurred during the days of Charles II (1660–1685) in the resort city of Bath where many went for the ardent spirits and warm mineral baths. The exact moment of the name change was recorded in 1709 in *The Tatler* by Isaac Bickerstaffe:

> It happened that on a publick day a celebrated beauty of those times was in the Cross Bath, and one of the crowd of her admirers took a glass of the water in which the fair one stood and drank her health to the company. There was in the place a gay fellow, half fuddled, who offered to jump in, and swore though he liked not the liquor, he would have the toast. He was opposed in his resolution; yet this whim gave foundation to the present honour which is done to the lady we mention in our liquor, who has ever since been called a toast.*

Toasting became immensely popular during the seventeenth century. This was especially true in the British Isles. "To drink at table," wrote one Englishman, "without drinking to the health of some one special, would be considered drinking on the sly, and as an act of incivility."

Popularity bred excess. The English discovered the Scandinavian custom of drinking not just to everyone present but to all of one's *absent* friends as well. Suddenly, one did not have to limit oneself to the mere twenty drinks normally pledged at a party of twenty.

Each nation had its own customs—almost always excessive. In Scotland, for instance, it was the custom to drink sparingly during the meal, allow the women to withdraw to the drawing room, and then bring in a large punch bowl filled with whisky, hot water, and sugar. Goblets or mugs were used, and each round required a toast, a quick drink, and a turned-over vessel

---

* The Tatler, Vol. 1, No. 24.

to prove that all had been drunk. One scholar of the period wrote, "During the seventeenth and the earlier portion of the eighteenth century, after-dinner drinking was protracted for eight to ten hours."

On important occasions, the toaster mounted his chair, placed his right foot on the table and bellowed out a favorite sentiment—"May ne'er waur be amang us," "May the pleasures of the evening bear the reflection of the morning," or whatever. All of this was accompanied by lusty cheering.

The toasting and hoisting that accompanied Scotch weddings were enough to put a cramp in the arm. According to an account from 1692, the process began when the parents of the bride and groom met to make the wedding arrangements. The two families would meet at a point equidistant between their two homes and if all went well, they would bring an agreement bottle of whisky with which the coming wedding would be toasted. Closer to the actual event was the predecessor of today's bachelor party. The male friends of the bride and the male friends of the groom would meet halfway between the bride's and the groom's houses. Each group would appoint a "champion" and the two men would race, either on horseback or foot, to the bride's house where the winner would receive a beribboned bottle. The bottle would be brought back to be passed among the assembled men as they drank to the bride's health. Then came the wedding and more toasting and drinking.

This period also witnessed some strange toasting customs. One practice called for men to show their affection for a woman by stabbing themselves in the arm, mixing their blood in their wine, and drinking to the lady in question. The Prince of Morocco in Shakespeare's *The Merchant of Venice* alludes to this when he talks of making "an incision for your love," and a song of the time rightly proclaimed,

> I stabbed my arm to drink her health,
> The more fool I, the more fool I.

No less repulsive was the custom, prevalent among students of the period, of proving one's love by toasting in imaginative but progressively nauseating concoctions. In his *History of Toasting*, Richard Valpy French tells of two Oxford students grossly proving their devotion to a beauty named Molly: "One, determined to prove that his love did not stick at trifles, took a spoonful of soot, mixed it with his wine, and drank off the mixture. His companion, determined not to be outdone, brought from his closet a phial of ink, which he drank, exclaiming, 'To triumph and Miss Molly.'"

As if this were not enough, student innovators of the time also first hit upon the wretched business of grabbing a woman's shoe, using it to ladle wine from a common bowl, and toasting the shoe's owner. Neither the shoe nor the wine benefited.

Though this was not a time of great subtlety, there was an occasional hint of it. The outlawed Jacobites would publicly, though secretly, drink to their exiled Stuart monarch, Bonnie Prince Charlie, by passing their glass over a bowl of water. Thus, while ostensibly toasting the Hanoverian King George II, they were actually drinking to "the king across the water." Less subtle was this Jacobite toast:

> God bless the King, I mean the Faith's Defender,
> God bless—no harm in blessing—the Pretender,
> But which is Pretender, and which is King?
> God bless us all! that's quite another thing.

If anything, it appears that toasting became even more pervasive during the boozy eighteenth and early nineteenth centuries. New institutions emerged, most notably the position of toastmaster. In Henry Fielding's *Tom Jones*, published in 1749, there is reference to a toastmaster whose duties were to propose and announce toasts. In those days the duties of the toastmaster tended to be refereelike in that his main function was to give all toasters a fair chance to make their contribution. Then, as now, the prime rule of toastmastering was to keep sober and offend nobody.

For the most part, the toasts of this period tended to be short, crisp, and to the point—or as one student of toasting has put it, "these were not an excuse for speeches but for wit and wine." A case in point were the toasts that were given in the officer's wardroom during the days when Horatio Nelson commanded the English navy. The first toast would always be to the king with the second (changing each day) prescribed as follows:

MONDAY:	"Our ships at sea."
TUESDAY:	"Our men."
WEDNESDAY:	"Ourselves."
THURSDAY:	"A bloody war or a sickly season."
FRIDAY:	"A willing foe and sea room."
SATURDAY:	"Sweethearts and wives."
SUNDAY:	"Absent friends."

In contrast, the toasts of the era's sailors were more poetic:

The wind that blows, the ship that goes
And the lass that loves a sailor.

Damn his eyes,
If he ever tries
To rob a poor man of his ale.

If the toasts were frugal, the drinking that went with them was anything but. In Dyott's *Diary 1781–1845* an account is given of a dinner at which the prince regent, afterward George IV, was one of the celebrants.

The Prince took the chair himself and ordered me to be his Vice. We had a very good dinner and he sent wine of his own, the very best Claret I ever tasted. We had the Grenadiers drawn up in front of the mess-room windows to fire a volley in honour of the toasts. As soon as dinner was over he began. He did not drink himself: he always drinks Madeira. He took very good care to see everybody fill, and he gave 23 bumpers without a halt. In the course of my experience I never saw such fair drinking. When he had finished his list of bumpers, I begged leave as Vice to give the Superior, and recommended it to the Society to stand up on our chairs with three times three, taking their time from the Vice. I think it was the most laughable sight I ever beheld to see our Governor, our General, and the Commodore all so drunk they could scarce stand on the floor, hoisted up on their chairs with each a bumper in his hand; and the three times three cheers was what they were afraid to attempt for fear of falling. I then proposed his Royal Highness and a good wind whenever he sailed (he intended sailing on Monday) with the same ceremony. He stood at the head of the table during both these toasts, and I never saw a man laugh so in my life. When we had drunk the last, the old Governor desired to know if we had any more as he said if once he got down he should never get up again. His Royal Highness saw we were all pretty well done, and he walked off. There were twenty dined, we drank sixty-three bottles of wine.

There is ample evidence to suggest that such excess was as common in America. One account from New York in 1770 describes a dinner held for a Captain McDougal and forty-four of his friends. They used forty-five pounds of steak and drank forty-five toasts. A description of a New York dinner in 1787 tells of the diners toasting their way through fifteen kinds of wine and two beers.

In fact, nobody seemed to have a lock on such behavior. A custom which became popular in Edinburgh in the nineteenth century was known as "saving the ladies." Lord Cockburn described the custom in his *Journals*:

When after any fashionable assembly the male guests had conducted their fair partners to their homes, they returned to the supper-room. Then one of the number would drink to the health of the lady he professed to admire, and in so doing empty his glass. Another gentleman would name another lady, also drinking a bumper in her honour. The former would reply by swallowing a social glass to his lady, followed by the other, each combatant persisting till one of the two fell upon the floor. Other couples followed in like fashion. These drinking competitions were regarded with interest by gentlewomen who next morning enquired as to the prowess of their champions.

Cockburn, by the way, was literally horrified by the inane and sentimental lines that his contemporaries would utter as "an excuse for the glass." Some of the toasts which most disgusted him were: "May the hand of charity wipe away the tears from the eyes of sorrow," "May the pleasure of the evening bear the reflections of the morning," and, saving the worst for last, "The reflection of the moon in the cawn bosom of the lake."

Over the years such excesses prompted more than a few decrees, rulings, and antitoast crusades. This opposition is worthy of a moment's digression.

Among others, Charles the Great, Maximilian, and Charles V enacted laws against the vice. Even Louis XIV, not one to be put off by a touch of debauchery, finally forbade the offering of toasts at his court. It is noteworthy that one of the main objectives of the first known temperance society (founded in 1517) was the abolition of the custom of toasting. In the American Colonies, a law was put into effect in Massachusetts in 1634 that banned the custom of drinking to another's health, a practice that was deemed an "abominable . . . useless ceremony." (The law, largely ignored, was repealed in 1645.) In England a small legion of moralists, politicians, and religious leaders opposed toasting and its attendant evils. In 1713, for instance, the Bishop of Cork became so upset with the practice of drinking to the dead that he issued both a stern injunction and a widely distributed pamphlet against it. Typical of the attacks on the custom was this injection from Lord Chief Justice Sir Matthew Hale, which was written for his grandchildren.

> I will not have you begin, or pledge any health, for it is become one of the greatest artifices of drinking and occasions of quarrelling in the Kingdom. If you pledge another, and a third, and so onward; and if you pledge as many as will be drank, you must be debauched and drunk. If they will needs know the reason for your refusal, it is fair to answer: "That your grandfather who brought you up, from whom, under God, you have the estate you enjoy or expect, left this in command with you, that you should never begin or pledge a health."

Of all those who crusaded against toasting, however, it would be hard to find one with a greater antagonism than William Prynne who, among other things, devoted a whole book to the link between the devil and the custom. The book, *Health's Sicknesse*, was published in 1628 and alleges that "the great, Deuill-god Jupiter was the first inventer, founder, and instituter of our Hellish and Heathenish Healthes." At another point he asserts "that this drinking and quaffing of healthes had its origin and birth from Pagans, heathens, and infidels, yea, from the very Deuill himself; that it is but a worldly, carnall, prophane, nay, heathenish and deuillish custom, which sauors of nothing else but Paganisme."

Prynne was certainly true to his convictions and not one to backslide at a party. On June 6, 1664, as recorded in his *Diary*, Samuel Pepys attended a dinner at which Prynne "would not drink any health, no, not the King's but sat down with his hat on all the while; but nobody took notice of him at all."

Interestingly, Prynne is hardly alone in his antitoast writing. Ranging from St. Augustine ("this filthy and unhappy custom of drinking healths") up through the beginning of this century, a great body of literature has been amassed against the custom. In fact, the most thorough book on the subject, *The History of Toasting* by the Reverend Richard Valpy French, is written by a man who despised toasting. Though scrupulously factual, French delights in bringing to light gruesome, bloody episodes in which toasting took place. He outdoes himself in telling of an ancient Danish ballad:

> In one very old one, a husband after treacherously murdering his wife's twelve brothers during their sleep, and whilst they were his guests, fills a cup with their blood, which he brings to his wife that she might pledge him in it. Many years after, the wife, in retaliation, whilst her husband's relations are visiting him, steals out of bed at dead of night, murders them all, fills a cup with their gore, returns to her husband's chamber, and whilst he still sleeps securely, ties him hand and foot. She then wakes him, and after mockingly asking him to pledge her in the cup of blood, dispatches him. At that moment their baby in its cradle wakes up and cries out, so the mother, fearing lest in afterlife her son should avenge his father's murder, makes matters safe by quietly dashing its brains out.

French also uncovered such things as an ancient tribe, "the old Guebres," who exposed the corpses of their parents to the "fowls of the air," then reserved only the skulls from the decay and fashioned cups from them.

Such skulduggery notwithstanding, there were those who promoted toasting as a blessing, as an amenity and a graceful custom with, as one Victorian writer put it, "a quality as pleasant as a handshake, as warm as a kiss."

An early—if not the earliest—book entirely devoted to toasts and toasting is J. Roach's *The Royal Toastmaster,* published in London in 1791. Roach was clearly intent on cleaning up the image of the custom. "Its use," he says of the toast, "is well known to all ranks, as a stimulative to hilarity, and an incentive to innocent mirth, to loyal truth, to pure morality and to mutual affection." At one point he ascribes great power to it:

A Toast or Sentiment very frequently excites good humor, and revives languid conversation; often does it, when
properly applied, cool the heat of resentment, and blunt the
edge of animosity. A well-applied Toast is acknowledged, uni-
versally, to sooth the flame of acrimony, when season and reason oft used their efforts to no purpose.

Roach laments "former times" and to some extent the "contemporary custom" of banning women from toasting sessions.
In introducing his book of "decent toasts" he points out that the
reason women were often excluded is the indecency of many
toasts and the general climate of "boisterous and illiberal mirth."
    If nothing else, Roach did help set a new tone. His toasts
were predictably proper ("Confusion to the minions of vice!"
and "May reason be the pilot when passion blows the gale!") and
politically liberal in the modern sense ("To the abolition of the
slave trade," "The rights of man!" and, incredibly for 1791 England, "The liberty of North America!").
    Another early collection of toasts was *The Toastmaster's Guide*
by T. Hughes, which was published in London in 1806. Like
Roach, Hughes favored the quick one-liner of the time; but
unlike Roach, he was not above a little early-nineteenth-century
spice with his toasts. A sampling from Hughes's collection:

The two that makes a third.
The rose of pleasure without the thorn.
The modest maid, who covered herself with her lover.
The commodity most thought of and least talk'd of.
Mirth, wine and love.
May the works of our nights never fear the day-light.
Old wine and young women.
Prudence and temperance with claret and champagne.
Love without fear, and life without care.
May we never want a friend to cheer us, or a bottle to
cheer him.
A generous heart and a miser's fortune.

Short shoes and long corns to the enemies of Great
Britain.
May we do as we would be done by.
May we live in pleasure and die out of debt.
A blush of detection to the lovers of deceit.
May British cuckolds never want horns.

Many short toasts that are still heard today—"Good luck
until we are tired of it!" "May poverty be a day's march behind
us!" "Champagne to our real friends and real pain to our sham
friends!"—appear in Hughes's book.

Toasting transferred easily to the United States, where the
Revolution and the newness of the nation were great inspira-
tions. During the war the toasts tended in the direction of curses:

> To the enemies of our country!
> May they have cobweb breeches, a porcupine saddle, a
> hard-trotting horse, and an eternal journey.

After the war no official dinner or celebration was complete
without thirteen toasts, one for each state. For many years, the
thirteen toasts were obligatory at local Fourth of July celebra-
tions. At such times each toast was followed by an artillery salute,
three cheers from the crowd, and a song.

Although the exact toasts differed somewhat from locale to
locale, they were generally always patriotic, proud, and nonpar-
tisan. They were dedicated to things ranging from the holiday
itself ("May it ever be held in grateful remembrance by the
American people") to the nation's former presidents ("In the
evenings of well-spent lives pleased with the fruits of their labors, they cheerfully await the summons that shall waft them to
brighter abodes.") Invariably, there was a toast to the signers of
the Declaration of Independence:

> From this act of treason against the British Crown sprang a
> chart of Liberty and Emancipation broad as the universe and
> filled with glad tiding and a good will towards men. They who
> perilled their lives by this noble act will live and be cherished in
> the hearts of free men.

· · ·

The origin of the thirteen toasts appears to date from the series of banquets held in honor of George Washington on his retirement. At one such banquet in Annapolis, Washington added a fourteenth of his own: "Sufficient Powers to Congress for general purposes!" The custom of the thirteen toasts has been all but forgotten, but was recently revived at the Genesse Country Museum in Mumford, New York, as part of the local Fourth of July observation.

Toasting not only transferred easily to North America but was enhanced by the skill of various practitioners including some of America's early leaders. If not the best, Benjamin Franklin certainly ranked with them. A number of his toasts have been recalled but none more often than one he delivered at Versailles while American emissary to France. On this occasion the toasting was led off by the British ambassador, who said, "George the Third, who, like the sun in its meridian, spreads a luster throughout and enlightens the world." The next toast came from the French minister, who said, "The illustrious Louis the Sixteenth, who, like the moon, sheds his mild and benevolent rays on and influences the globe." Franklin finished the round: "George Washington, commander of the American armies, who, like Joshua of old, commanded the sun and the moon to stand still, and both obeyed."

Other influences were at work in the transfer of the custom to America. Around 1800 there was a high-spirited drinking club in London known as the Anacreontic Society, which met at the Crown and Anchor tavern. It was named for the Greek poet Anacreon, who was known for poems that praised love and wine. Each meeting opened with a singing toast "To Anacreon in Heaven," which ended with these joyous lines:

> While thus we agree,
> Our toast let it be.
> May our club flourish happy, united and free!
> And long may the sons of Anacreon entwine,
> The myrtle of Venus with Bacchus's vine!

The composition became popular enough that a number of Americans learned it. On several occasions the tune was used to accommodate lyrics written in America. One of these writers was Francis Scott Key, who found it the perfect vehicle for his "Star-Spangled Banner."

If there was a Golden Age for toasting it came during the period from approximately 1880 to 1920. Scores of toast books and pamphlets came on the market, prominent authors wrote and contributed their own for anthologies, newspapers ran columns of them, and one periodical, *The National Magazine*, actually had its own Toast Editor, whose duties included judging the winners of its monthly toasting contest. Several writers of the period, such as Fred Emerson Brooks and Minna Thomas Antrim, built considerable reputations as toast writers, and the great comic poets of the time, like Oliver Herford and Wallace Irvin, created dozens of marvelous invitations to drink. One of Herford's many champagne toasts: "The bubble winked at me and said, 'You'll miss me, brother, when you're dead.' "

Toasts were written for every imaginable institution and situation—cities, colleges, states, holidays, baseball teams, fools, failures, short people, and fat people. A British collection contained a toast, several pages in length, written for "The Opening of an Electric Generating Station." Occupational toasts were very popular, and some clubs and fraternal organizations opened their dinners with a toast to each of the professions represented at the table. Many of these incorporated one or more atrocious pun. Thus almost everyone was given his due:

> **The Grocer:** Whosehonestteaisthebestpolicy! Or, May we spring up like vegetables, have turnip-noses, reddish cheeks, and carroty hair, and may our hearts never be hard, like those of cabbages, nor may we be rotten at the core.
> **The Paper Hanger:** Who is always up against it and still remains stuck up!
> **The Conductor:** May he always know what is fare!
> **The Author:** The queerest of animals; their tales come out of their heads!

. . .

The Baker: Who loafs around all day and still makes the dough!

The Glazier: Who takes panes to see his way through life!

The Well-Digger: Always feel above your business, and be glad of the fact that you do not have to begin at the bottom and work to the top!

Undertakers: May they never overtake us!

Blacksmiths: Success to forgery!

The Painter: When we work in the wet may we never want for dryers.

And the humble shoemaker was blessed with a host of toasts: He's a stick to the last. . . . He left his awl. . . . He pegged out. . . . He was well-heeled, but lost his sole. . . . He was on his uppers.

This was also a time for longer, more elaborate toasts. Some were long, florid, and overblown, which no doubt put to sleep as many as were entertained. Some of these toast-essays, however, had some punch, such as this one that took first prize in one of the *National Magazine*'s contests for 1911. The toast, entitled "The Way of a Woman," was submitted by Miss Saidee Lewis and went on for many lines until it came to this concluding paragraph:

"Of those marriageable misses, thinking life all love and kisses, mist and moonshine, glint and glamour, stardust borrowed from the skies! Man's a gross and sordid lummox—men are largely made of stomachs, and the songs of all the sirens will not take the place of pies!"

There were also political and military toasts of near epic proportions. An anti-Teddy Roosevelt toast, "No! Teddy Don't Play Fair," drones on for eleven stanzas before it gets to the point:

> But honest old Bill Bryan,
> With kindliness will wear
> Away all Republican lyin'
> No! Teddy don't play fair.

Ironically, a number of toasts were written in honor of the teetotaler Bryan, who nonetheless managed in social situations. Bryan once found himself in a position where he was called on to toast the British navy. He lifted his glass of water and said, "Gentlemen, I believe your victories were won on water."

A toast written in honor of Alton B. Parker after his unsuccessful bid for the presidency in 1904 is also typical of the period—if nothing else, it rhymes:

> It's a pardonable pride a Democrat feels
> For Alton B. Parker, Court of Appeals,
> He bore our standard last campaign,
> And although his fight was in vain,
> Alton B. Parker, you're alright.
> Alton B. Parker, may your skies be bright.

When Prohibition went into effect in 1920, the drinking continued, but the customs changed. A writer who was trying to reintroduce toasting and other traditional drinking customs in 1934 after repeal put it this way: "When Prohibition placed its stranglehold on our nation, it doomed for more than thirteen years the real art and etiquette of drinking."

Not only were wine, beer, and spirits on the banned list, but so for all practical purposes were the formularies, books, ads, and magazine articles that helped carry the lore and customs of drinking. A good bootlegger could get a few bottles of champagne (or a reasonable facsimile) for a wedding, but no publishers were bootlegging collections of wedding toasts. Banquets, large open parties, and many of the other functions where one used to go to have a drink or two and launch a few toasts were now scarce and usually dry. Places where one would go for a leisurely drink to toast the health of a friend's new baby—the corner saloon, the cocktail lounge, and the hotel bar—were shut down for the duration and replaced by dank speakeasies where one would slink to have a fast drink of questionable origin.

All of this is not to say that people did not toast, but in many cases their toasts' substance had to do with the Volstead Act, the antisaloonists, and the quality of bathtub gin. For example:

> Here's to Prohibition,
> The devil take it!
> They've stolen our wine,
> So now we make it.

At the very moment of repeal there was a lot of toasting, which for the most part was addressed to the act itself; but after this initial flurry, the custom of the toast continued the decline begun during Prohibition. There were, of course, many who continued the tradition, and from time to time new toasts appeared as did these two examples respectively from the 1930s and 1950s:

> Here's to the new radio—
> Here's to our neighbor's loudspeaker
> So loud we need none of our own
> May its volume never grow weaker.

> Here's to today!
> For tomorrow we may be radioactive.

Fortunately, there have been a few who have gone against the trend, so all is not lost. Like those who carried the seeds of the Renaissance through the time of Darkness, and like others who have gone against the cultural tide, we have:

THE MCELVY LEGACY. When New Yorker Douglas McElvy passed away in 1973, he left $12,000 for friends to toast him on the anniversary of his death. The cash lasted for three years, but according to reports in the papers his friends still meet each

New Year's Day at the bar where the legacy was drained to pour him a memorial gin and tonic and toast his empty stool.

THE COSGROVIANS. A society of self-styled bons vivants who for some years assembled each month in Washington, D.C., to honor the memory of an ardent Prohibitionist named Cosgrove who left water-dispensing monuments to the abstemious spirit. The Cosgrovian's toast: "Temperance. I'll drink to that!"

THE MCGOWAN INFLUENCE. If there is one place in the world today where the custom is doing well, it is Ireland. Jack McGowan, an affable man with the sponsorship of the Irish Distillers International in Dublin, has collected toasts and Irish blessings over the years. He shares this treasury with interested parties in so-called civilized areas of the world where the custom is presently out of style. Toasts from McGowan's collection have shown up in American newspaper columns and form the bulk of the section of this book containing Irish toasts.

SUMMIT TALK. Then there is the business of *glasnost* and the changing relationships between the United States and the Soviet Union. This thawing and warming has been accompanied by so much toasting that the *Washington Post's* headline the morning after the historic October 1990 Gorbachev-Bush dinner at the Soviet Embassy in Washington was TOASTED INSIDE AND OUT AT THE SOVIET EMBASSY. These toasts actually featured a degree of levity such as George Bush's to the two leaders' previous meetings anchored off the coast of the island nation of Malta: "[To] the memories of the days we spent in Malta—friendship, cooperation, seasick pills . . . ."

How to Use This Book

This book has been designed for both quick access and leisurely browsing. To accomplish both these ends, all of the toasting topics, and the toasts gathered under those topics, have been alphabetized. So that anyone looking for Hints for Effective Toasting, a collection of Historic Toasts as well as toasts having to with Health, Home, or Husbands will be rewarded by looking under *H*. *L* yields Love, Luck, and Lust in that order—a good toast right there.

The contents and generous use of "see also's" conspire to help you find appropriate toasts quickly, which in turn should make you rich, famous, and popular beyond your wildest dreams.

Toasts
and Toasting

A man is only as old as the woman he feels.

—GROUCHO MARX

Do not resist growing old—many are denied the privilege.

Fill high the goblet! Envious time steals, as we speak, our fleeting prime.

Here's a health to the future;
   A sigh for the past;
We can love and remember,
   And hope to the last,
And for all the base lies

That the almanacs hold
While there's love in the heart,
 We can never grow old.

Here's hoping that you live forever
And mine is the last voice you hear.

—WILLARD SCOTT *from*
A Gentleman's Guide to Toasting

Here's that we may live to eat the hen
That scratches on our grave.

I've never known a person to live to 110 or more, and then
die, to be remarkable for anything else.

—JOSH BILLINGS

Let him live to be a hundred! We want him on earth.

—OLIVER WENDELL HOLMES
to a friend

Long life to you and may you die in your own bed.

May our lives, like the leaves of the maple, grow
 More beautiful as they fade.
May we say our farewells, when it's time to go,
 All smiling and unafraid.

—LARRY E. JOHNSON

May the Lord love us but not call us too soon.

May virtue and truth
Guide you in youth
Catnip and sage
Cheer your old age.

—*Found in a geography book dated 1880,
Cuttingsville, Vermont*

May we keep a little of the fuel of youth to warm our body in old age.

May you enter heaven late.

May you live as long as you want, may you never want as long as you live.

May you live to be a hundred—and decide the rest for yourself.

Noah was six hundred years old before he knew how to build an ark—don't lose your grip.

—ELBERT HUBBARD

Oh to be seventy again!

—OLIVER WENDELL HOLMES, JR. *(on
the occasion of his passing a pretty girl on
the street at the age of about eighty-five*)

Only the young die good.

—OLIVER HERFORD

The good die young—here's hoping that you may live to a ripe old age.

To maturity:
  When there's snow on the roof,
  there's fire in the furnace.

To the Old Guard, the older we grow,
The more we take and the less we know.
At least the young men tell us so,
But the day will come, when they shall know
Exactly how far a glass can go,
To win the battle, 'gainst age, the foe.
Here's youth . . . in a glass of wine.

—JAMES MONROE MCLEAN,
The Book of Wine

To the old, long life and treasure;
To the young, all health and pleasure.

—BEN JONSON

You're not as young as you used to be
But you're not as old as you're going to be
So watch it!

—Irish

SEE ALSO: Birthdays; Health; New Years

31

alliterative

An alphabetical selection of this long-popular toast form. Many of these were regarded as old at the time of the American Revolution. Included at the end are two toast oddities in one: an orderly Jacobite offering and an acrostic.

Abundance, abstinence, and annihilation.
Abundance to the poor,
Abstinence to the intemperate,
Annihilation to the wicked.

Bachelors, banns, and buns.
Bachelors for the maidens,
Banns* for the bachelors,
Buns after the consummation of the banns.

Cheerfulness, content, and competency.
Cheerfulness in our cups,
Content in our minds,
Competency in our pockets.

The three good C's: conscience, claret, and cash.

Firmness, freedom, and fortitude.
Firmness in the Senate,
Freedom on the land,
Fortitude on the waves.

* Banns: the stated intention to marry.

Friendship, feeling, and fidelity.
Friendship without interest,
Feeling to our enemies,
Fidelity to our friends.

The three H's: Health, Honor, and Happiness.
Health to all the world,
Honor to those who seek for it,
Happiness in our homes.

The eight H's:
Handsome Husband,
Handsome House,
Health and Happiness,
Here and Hereafter.

Love, life, and liberty.
Love pure,
Life long,
Liberty boundless.

Mirth, music, and moderation.
Mirth at every board,
Music in all instruments,
Moderation in our desires.

Wine, wit, and wisdom.
Wine enough to sharpen wit,
Wit enough to give zest to wine,
Wisdom enough to "shut down" at the right time.

The following, known as the Jacobite Toast, is ascribed to Lord Duff who presented it in the year 1745.

A B C . . . A Blessed Change.

D E F . . . Down Every Foreigner.

G H J . . . Good Help James.

K L M . . . Keep Lord Marr.

N O P . . . Noble Ormond Preserve.

Q R S . . . Quickly Resolve Stewart.

T U V W . . . Truss Up Vile Whigs.

X Y Z . . . 'Xert Your Zeal.

anniversaries

Here is to loving, to romance, to us.
May we travel together through time.
We alone count as none, but together we're one,
For our partnership puts love to rhyme.

—Irish

Here's to you both—
a beautiful pair,
on the birthday
of your love affair.

Let anniversaries come and let anniversaries go—but may your happiness continue on forever.

Love seems the swiftest, but it is the slowest of growths. No man or woman really knows what perfect love is until they have been married a quarter of a century.

—MARK TWAIN

May the warmth of our affections survive the frosts of age.

To your coming anniversaries—may they be outnumbered only by your coming pleasures.

We've holidays and holy days, and memory days galore;
And when we've toasted every one, I offer just one more.
So let us lift our glasses high, and drink a silent toast—
The day, deep buried in each heart, that each one loves the most.

With fifty years between you
  and your well-kept wedding vow.
The Golden Age, old friends of mine,
  is not a fable now.

                    —The Golden Wedding at Longwood *by*
                       JOHN GREENLEAF WHITTIER

SEE ALSO: *Weddings*

A baby will make love stronger, days shorter, nights longer,
bankroll smaller, home happier, clothes shabbier, the past
forgotten, and the future worth living for.

A new life begun,
Like father, like son.

                                                    —*Irish*

Like one, like the other,
Like daughter, like mother.

                                                    —*Irish*

A generation of children on the children of your children.

                                                    —*Irish*

A lovely being scarcely formed or molded,
A rose with all its sweetest leaves yet folded.

                                        —LORD BYRON

Every baby born into the world is a finer one than the last.

—CHARLES DICKENS,
Nicholas Nickleby

Father of fathers, make me one,
A fit example for a son.

—DOUGLAS MALLOCH'S toast
for fathers with a son or sons

Grandchildren are gifts of God.
It is God's way . . .
Of compensating us for growing old.

—*Irish*

Here's to the baby—man to be—
May he be as fine as thee!
Here's to baby—woman to be—
May she be as sweet as thee!

Here's to the stork,
A most valuable bird,
That inhabits the residence districts.
He doesn't sing tunes,

Nor yield any plumes,
But he helps the vital statistics.

May he/she grow twice as tall as yourself and half as wise.

—*Irish*

So that our children will have wealthy parents.

"The stork has brought a little peach!"
  The nurse said with an air.
"I'm mighty glad," the father said.
  "He didn't bring a pear."

We haven't all the good fortune to be ladies; we have not all
been generals, or poets or statesmen; but when the toast
works down to the babies we stand on common ground. We've
all been babies.

—MARK TWAIN

SEE ALSO: *Parents*

Ale's a strong wrestler,
Flings all it hath met;
And makes the ground slippery,
Though it not be wet.

Beer! Beer! Beer!
We students do adore you,

Beer! Beer! Beer!
We love to see you foam;
When we for wine abjure you,
We miss you we assure you,
For it's only with clear sparkling beer
That students feel at home.

Come, sit we by the fireside
And roundly drink we hear,
Till that we see our cheeks all dyed
And noses tanned with beer.

—ROBERT HERRICK

Here's to the best ale in the best ale.

—MR. PICKWICK, *from* Pickwick Papers
by Charles Dickens

"Let No Man Thirst For Lack Of Real Ale."

—*Matchbook toast from
the Commonwealth Brewing Co., Boston,
Massachusetts*

Let's drink the liquid of amber so bright;
Let's drink the liquid with foam snowy white;
Let's drink the liquid that brings all good cheer;
Oh, where is the drink like old-fashioned beer?

—*A popular nineteenth-century toast often
adapted to the use of a particular brand
whose name was substituted for
"old-fashioned" in the last line.*

None so deaf as those who will not hear.
None so blind as those who will not see.
But I'll wager none so deaf nor blind that he
Sees not nor hears me say come drink this beer.

—W. L. HASSOLDT

Show me a nation whose national beverage is beer, and I'll show you an advanced toilet technology.

—MARK HAWKINS *in the* New York Times,
September 25, 1977

Who'd care to be a bee and sip
Sweet honey from the flower's lip
When he might be a fly and steer
Head first into a can of beer?

SEE ALSO: *Libations; Revelry; Spirits*

A speedy calm to the storms of life.

All of this has been a religious experience: a living hell.

Bury the blue devils.*

* The old, original version is longer: Come fill the bowl, each jolly soul; Let Bacchus guide our revels; Join cup to lip, with "hip, hip, hip," And bury the blue devils.

Everybody in life gets the same amount of ice. The rich get it in the summer and the poor in the winter.

—*Words found in the typewriter of sportswriter Bat Masterson after he suffered a fatal heart attack.*

Here's a health to poverty; it sticks by us when our friends forsake us.

Here's to thee my honest friend,
Wishing these hard times to mend.

If the world is going wrong,
  Forget it!
Sorrow never lingers long—
  Forget it!
If your neighbor bears ill-will,
If your conscience won't be still,
If you owe an ancient bill,
  Forget it!

If this is a blessing, it is certainly *very* well disguised.

—WINSTON CHURCHILL *on his defeat in the 1945 general election, quoted by Richard Nixon in* Memoirs of Richard Nixon.

Laugh and the world laughs with you;
Weep, and it gives you the laugh anyway.

Let us make our glasses kiss;
Let us quench the sorrow-cinders.

—RALPH WALDO EMERSON, *in* The Persian of Hafiz, *1851*

May poverty always be a day's march behind us.

May the morning of prosperity shine on the evening of adversity.

May the sunshine of comfort dispel the clouds of despair.

May we ever be able to part with our troubles to advantage.

Remember the poor—it costs nothing.

—JOSH BILLINGS

The right time and place is coming for you, don't let it pass.

—*Fortune cookie message*

To the Great Unknown—who is waiting to do us a favor.

Troubles like babies grow larger by nursing.
Worry is rust upon the blade.

—HENRY WARD BEECHER

SEE ALSO: *General; Luck; Past, Present, and Future*

The Bible does not give us any direct mention of toasting, but there are a number of passages that indicate that the custom was observed. Even an antitoast cleric of the last century had to concede: "It is hardly probable that Ben-hadad and the thirty-two kings, his companions, would drink themselves drunk in the pavilions without some interchange of courtesies" (see 1 Kings 20:16).

A number of lines from the Bible have been used as toasts including these:

A feast is made for laughter, and wine maketh merry.

—*Ecclesiastes* 10:19

Do not arouse or awaken love
until it so desires.

—*Song of Solomon* 2.7

Drink no longer water, but use a
little wine for thy stomach's sake.

—1 *Timothy* 5:23

*Eat thy bread with joy, and drink thy
wine with a merry heart.*

—*Ecclesiastes* 9:7

Forsake not an old friend, for the new is not comparable to
him. A new friend is as new wine: when it is old, thou shalt
drink it with pleasure.

—*Ecclesiastes* 9:10

Give . . . wine unto those that be of heavy heart.

—*Proverbs* 31:6

The best wine . . . that goeth down sweetly, causing the lips of
those that are asleep to speak.

—*Song of Solomon* 7:9

Wine maketh glad the heart of man.

—*Psalms* 104:15

Wine nourishes, refreshes and cheers. Wine is the foremost
of all medicines . . . whenever wine is lacking, medicines
become necessary.

—*The Talmud*

Wine was created from the beginning to make men joyful, and not to make men drunk. Wine drunk with moderation is the joy of the soul and the heart.

—*Ecclesiastes* 31:35–36

Wine, which cheereth God and man.

—*Judges* 9:13

SEE ALSO: *Food*

A health, and many of them. Birthdays were never like this when I had 'em.

Although another year is past
He's/She's no older than the last!

Another candle on your cake?
Well, that's no cause to pout,
Be glad that you have strength enough
To blow the damn thing out.

Another year older? Think this way:
Just one day older than yesterday!

God grant you many and happy years,
  Till, when the last has crowned you,

The dawn of endless days appears,
  And heaven is shining round you!

Happy birthday to you
  And many to be,
With friends that are true
  As you are to me!

Here's to you! No matter how old you are, you don't
look it!

Many happy returns of the day of your birth:
Many blessings to brighten your pathway on earth;
Many friendships to cheer and provoke you to mirth;
Many feastings and frolics to add to your girth.

—ROBERT H. LORD

May you have been born on your lucky star and may that star
never lose its twinkle.

May you live to be a hundred years with one extra year to
repent.

—Irish

Time marches on!
Now tell the truth—
Where did you find
The fountain of youth?

To wish you joy on your birthday
And all the whole year through,
For all the best that life can hold
Is none too good for you.

To your birthday, glass held high,
Glad it's you that's older—not I.

SEE ALSO: *Age; Health*

This term for absurd contradictions—e.g., "It's a mighty good thing for your wife that you're not married"—goes back at least to the thirteenth century. Some that have become toasts:

A toast to posterity—though it does nothing for us.

Here's to abstinence—as long as it's practiced in moderation.

Here's to _____, equal to none.

Here's to the glorious _____, the last in the fight and the first out.

Here's to your wedding and many of them.

I hope you are all here to do honor to the toast. As many of ye as is present will say, "Here!" and as many of ye as is not present will say, "Absent!"

Liberty all over the world, and everywhere else.

May every patriot love his native country, whether he was born in it or not.

To our health. May it remain with us long after we die.

celia's toast

(with variations)

Drink to me only with thine eyes,
  And I will pledge with mine;
Or leave a kiss but in the cup,
  And I'll not look for wine.

—BEN JONSON, "To Celia"

Drink to me only with thine eyes,
  And I will pledge with mine;
For I would have to pledge my watch
  If she should drink more wine.

Drink to me only with thine eyes,
  And I will pledge with mine;
Or, leave a kiss within the cup—
  I'll wash it down with wine.

Drink to me only with thine eyes?
I'll take a little wine.
  The eyes we prize
  Are full of lies,
I'll none of that in mine.

champagne

Here's champagne to your real friends and real pain to our sham friends.

Here's to champagne, the drink divine,
That makes us forget all our troubles;
It's made of a dollar's worth of wine
And three dollars' worth of bubbles.*

If ever . . . in the eternal times that are to come, you and I shall sit down in Paradise, in some little shady corner by ourselves; and if we shall by any means be able to smuggle a basket of champagne there (I won't believe in a Temperance Heaven), and if we shall then cross our celestial legs in the celestial grass that is forever tropical, and strike our glasses and our heads together, till both musically ring in concert,—then, O my dear fellow-mortal, how shall we pleasantly discourse of all the things manifold which now so distress us,—when all the earth shall be but a reminiscence, yea, its final dissolution an antiquity.

—HERMAN MELVILLE *to*
Nathaniel Hawthorne

O thrice accursed
Be a champagne thirst,
When the price of beer's all we've got.

* This is the original version of this toast, at least ninety years old; so you may want to inflate the dollar amounts to update it.

48

Some take their gold
In minted mold,
And some in harps hereafter,
But give me mine
In bubbles fine
And keep the change in laughter.

—OLIVER HERFORD

The bubble winked at me and said,
"You'll miss me, brother, when you're dead."

—OLIVER HERFORD

To the glorious, golden vintage of France,
Whose bubbling beauties our spirits entrance;
When with friends tried and true this nectar we quaff
We wish for a neck like a thirsty giraffe.

SEE ALSO: *Wine; Libations; Revelry*

cheeses

Camembert

Soft, aromatic, ammoniacal,
Angelic half, half demoniacal;
We pledge thee, Camembert,
  The Rare:
Thou apotheosis of decay.

—W. E. P. FRENCH

Cheese—milk's leap toward immortality.

—CLIFTON FADIMAN

Limburger

The rankest compound of villainous smell
That ever offended nostril.

—SHAKESPEARE

Roquefort

The king of cheeses and the cheese of kings.

christmas

A Christmas wish—
May you never forget
what is worth remembering
or remember
what is best forgotten.

—*Irish*

A Merry Christmas this December
To a lot of folks I don't remember.

—FRANKLIN P. ADAMS, *1922*

"**A**s fits the holy Christmas birth,
  Be this, good friends, our carol still—
Be peace on earth, be peace on earth,
  To men of gentle will."

—WILLIAM MAKEPEACE THACKERAY

At Christmas play and make good cheer
For Christmas comes but once a year.

—THOMAS TUSSER

Be merry all, be merry all,
With holly dress the festive hall,
Prepare the song, the feast, the ball,
To welcome Merry Christmas.

"**B**lessed is the season which engages the whole world in a
conspiracy of love."

—HAMILTON WRIGHT MABIE

"**C**hristmas is here,
Merry old Christmas,
Gift-bearing, heart-touching, joy-bringing Christmas,
Day of grand memories, king of the year."

—WASHINGTON IRVING

"Heap on more wood!—the wind is chill
 But let it whistle as it will,
We'll keep our Christmas merry still."

Here's to the holly with its bright red berry.
Here's to Christmas, let's make it merry.

Here's to the day of good will, cold weather, and warm
hearts!

Here's to us all!
God bless us every one!

> *—Tiny Tim's toast,*
> *from* A Christmas Carol by CHARLES DICKENS

Or, for those who would like to savor the entire incident:

> At last the dinner was all done, the cloth cleared, the hearth
> swept, and the fire made up. The compound in the jug being
> tasted, and considered perfect, apples and oranges were put
> upon the table, and a shovelful of chestnuts on the fire. Then
> all the Cratchit family drew around the hearth in what Bob
> Cratchit called a circle, meaning half a one; and at Bob Crat-
> chit's elbow stood the family display of glass. Two tumblers
> and a custard-cup without a handle. These held the hot stuff
> from the jug, however, as well as golden goblets would have
> done; and Bob served it out with beaming looks, while the
> chestnuts on the fire sputtered and crackled noisily. Then Bob
> proposed:

"A Merry Christmas to us all, my dears. God bless us!"
Which the family re-echoed.
"God bless us every one!" said Tiny Tim, the last of all.

> —CHARLES DICKENS,
> A Christmas Carol

Here's wishing you more happiness
Than all my words can tell,
Not just alone for Christmas
But for all the year as well.

Holly and ivy hanging up
And something wet in every cup.

—Irish

I have always thought of Christmas as a good time; a kind,
forgiving, generous, pleasant time; a time when men and
women seem by one consent to open their hearts freely; and
so I say "God bless Christmas."

—CHARLES DICKENS

I know I've wished you this before
But every year I wish it more,
A Merry Christmas.

—From an old postcard

I wish you a Merry Christmas
And a Happy New Year
A pocket full of money
And a cellar full of beer!

Joy to the world—and especially to you.

May the Virgin and her Child lift your latch on Christmas
night.

—Irish. This refers to the old Irish custom
of leaving the door unbolted and a candle in the
window for Mary on her way to Bethlehem.

May you be as contented as Christmas finds you all the year
round.

May you be poor in misfortune this Christmas
and rich in blessings
slow to make enemies
quick to make friends
and rich or poor, slow or quick,
as happy as the New Year is long.

May you be the first house in the parish to
welcome St. Nicholas.

May you never be without a drop at Christmas.

May your corn stand high as yourself, your fields grow bigger
with rain, and the mare know its own way home on Christmas
night.

*May you live as long as you Wish, and have all you Wish as long as
you live. This is my Christmas Wish for you.*

May your sheep all have lambs but not on Christmas night.

Peace and plenty for many a Christmas to come.

Then let us be merry and taste the good cheer,
And remember old Christmas comes but once a year.

—*From an old Christmas carol*

'Twas the month after Christmas,
And Santa had flit;
Came there tidings for father
Which read: "Please remit!"

c u r s e s

A toast in reverse is a curse. In form, they are alike right down to the common openings of "Here's to . . ." and "May you. . . ." Here, in English, is a sampling largely drawn form the two great sources of malediction, Gaelic and Yiddish.

A plague on both your houses.

—SHAKESPEARE, Romeo and Juliet, *Act III*

Corns should grow on your nose.

—*Yiddish*

Here's to short shoes and long corns to our enemies.

—*Irish*

May a band of gypsies camp in your belly and train bears to dance on your liver.

—Yiddish

May all your enemies move in with you.

—Yiddish

May his cradle ne'er rock, may his box have no lock,
May his wife have no frock for to cover her back,
May his cock never crow, may his bellows ne'er blow,
And his pipe and his pot, may he ever more lack.

—Irish, a curse to an informer

May his pig never grunt, may his cat never hunt,
That a ghost may catch him in the dark of the night,
May his hen never lay, may his ass never bray,
And his goat fly away like an old paper kite.

—Irish

May his soul be forever tormented by fire and his bones be dug up by dogs and dragged through the streets of Minneapolis. . . .

—From Happy To Be Here *by Garrison Keillor*

May his spade never dig.
May his sow never pig.
May each hair in his wig be well thrashed with a flail.
May his door never latch.
May his turkeys not hatch.
May the rats eat his mail.

May every old fairy from Cork to Dunleary dip him snug
and airy in river or lake where the eel and the trout may
dine on the snout of the monster that murdered Nell
Flaherty's Drake.

—One verse of Irish cursing song "Nell
Flaherty's Drake"

May she marry a ghost, and bear him a kitten, and may the
high king of glory permit it to get the mange.

—Irish

May the devil cut the toes off all our foes, that we may know
them by their limping.

—Irish

May the devil make a ladder of your backbone while he is
picking apples in the garden of hell.

—Irish

May the greatest doctors in the world know of your case.

—Yiddish

May the seven seas not be enough for your enemas.

—Yiddish

May *you be alone in paradise.*

—Yiddish

May you be proof that a human being can endure anything.

—Yiddish

May you grow so rotten that goats, skunks, and pigs refuse to be near you.

—Yiddish

May you never develop stomach trouble from too rich a diet.

—Yiddish

May you never go to hell, but always be on your way.

—Yiddish

May you turn into a sparrow and owe your existence to the droppings of a horse.

—Yiddish

May your buttocks fall off.

—Yiddish

May your finger get stuck in your nose.

—Irish

May your nose run and your feet smell.

—Yiddish

May your retirement plan be supervised by Jimmy Hoffa.

—Steve Allen

May your sex life be as good as your credit.

—Yiddish

Pieces should fall off you.

—Yiddish

That all your teeth should fall out—but one should remain
for a toothache.

—Yiddish

You should grow like an onion with your feet in the air and
your head in the ground.

—Yiddish

You should have a child through the ribs.

—Yiddish

SEE ALSO: *Hell and Damnation*

Ah, make we the most of what we may yet spend,
Before we too into the Dust descend;
Dust into Dust, and under Dust to lie,
Sans wine, sans song, sans singer, and sans end.

—OMAR KHAYYÁM

All care to the wind we merrily fling,
For the damp, cold grave is a dead sure thing!
It's a dead sure thing we're alive tonight
And the damp, cold grave is out of sight.

—ERNEST JARROLD (*Toast of the Vampire
Club*)

Cause of Death: Life.

—TOM BOSWELL'S *epitaph for Bill Veeck,*
The Washington Post, *May 31, 1981*

Here's to death, because death will give me one last bier.

Life is a jest
   And all things show it;
I thought so once—
   But now I know it.

—JOHN GAY'S *epitaph, appearing on his*
grave in Westminster Abbey

May every hair on your head turn into a candle to light your
way to heaven, and may God and His Holy Mother take the
harm of the years away from you.

—Irish

May we all come to peaceful ends,
And leave our debts unto our friends.

Oh, here's to other meetings,
   And merry greetings then;
And here's to those we've drunk with,
   But never can again.

Over their hallowed graves may the winds of heaven whisper hourly benedictions.

She drank good ale, good punch and wine
And lived to the age of 99.

—*Epitaph for Rebecca Freeland at Edwalton, Notts, 1741*

Take lightly that which heavy lies;
what all respect, do you despair;
some flippancy your soul may save.
—A goose is walking on your grave.

—*"Motto," by artist Peggy Bacon, quoted in "Peggy Bacon's World," the* Boston Globe, *July 8, 1979*

Though life is now pleasant and sweet to the sense
We'll be damnably mouldy a hundred years hence.

—*Old pirate toast*

Time cuts down all,
Both great and small.

'Tis my will when I die, not a tear shall be shed,
No *Hic Jacet* be graved on my stone,
But pour o'er my coffin a bottle of red,
And write that *His Drinking is Done.*

To Death, the jolly old bouncer, now
    Our glasses let's be clinking;
If he hadn't put other out, I trow,
    To-night we'd not be drinking.

—OLIVER HERFORD

To live in hearts we leave behind is not to die.

Wash me when dead in the juice of the vine, dear
friends! Let your funeral service be drinking and wine, dear
   friends!
And if you would meet again when the
Doomsday comes, Search the dust of the tavern, and sift from
   it mine, dear friends!
We toast his roguish and venerable shade.

—JAMES J. KILPATRICK'S *toast to H. L.*
Mencken on the 101st anniversary of
Mencken's birth, Quoted in the Baltimore
Sun, *September 13, 1981.*

Daddy Neptune, one day, to Freedom did say,
If ever I lived upon dry land,
The spot I would hit on would be little Britain!
Says Freedom, "Why that's my own island!"
O, it's a snug little island!
A right little, tight little island!
Search the world round, none can be found
So happy as this little island.

England! my country, great and free!
Heart of the world, I drink to thee!

First pledge our Queen this solemn night,
  Then drink to England, every guest;
That man's the best Cosmopolite
  Who loves his native country best.

—SIR ALFRED TENNYSON, Hands All Round

In English beer,
With an English cheer,
To the right little,
Tight little island!

O England!—model to thy inward greatness,
Like little body with a mighty heart.

—SHAKESPEARE, King Henry V, *Act II*

Our friends are coming, our friends are coming.

—*From Vice President George Bush's toast at*
the British embassy, during the visit of the
Prince and Princess of Wales, November 11, 1985.

St. George he was for England,
And before he killed the dragon
He drank a pint of English ale
Out of an English flagon.

—G. K. CHESTERTON

He is an Englishman!
For he himself hath said it,
And it's greatly to his credit,
That he is an Englishman!
For he might have been a Roosian,
A French, or Turk, or Proosian,
Or perhaps Itali-an!
But in spite of all temptations,
To belong to other nations,
He remains an Englishman!

—W. S. GILBERT

Old England is our home, and Englishmen are we;
Our tongue is known in every clime, our flag on every sea.

—MARY HOWITT

To the land of Chaucer and Shakespeare.

—OLIVE SCHREINER

To England

Now, island Empress, wave they crest on high,
And bid the banner of the Patron flow,
Gallant St. George, the flower of Chivalry,
For thou hast faced him like a dragon foe,
And rescued innocence from overthrow,
And trampled down like him, tyrannic might,
And to the gazing world mayst proudly show
The chosen emblem of thy sainted knight,
Who quell'd devouring pride, and vindicated right!

—SIR WALTER SCOTT

To the Mother of the English-speaking race.

Undaunted in peril and foremost in danger,
Ever ready the rights of mankind to defend,
The guard of the weak and support of the stranger;
To oppression a foe, and to freedom a friend.
Amid the rude scenes of dismay and commotion,
Since Anarchy first her red banner unfurled,
Still firm as a rock, in her own native ocean,
Stood England, the Anchor and Hope of the world.

—COBB

To Great Britain

Britain's myriad voices call,
Sons, be welded, each and all
Into one imperial whole;
One with Britain heart and soul,
One fleet, one flag, one life, one throne—
Britons, hold your own!

—TENNYSON

"excuses for the glass"

In Richard Brinsley Sheridan's comedy The School for Scandal, *Sir Toby Bumper recites a toast that thereafter defined a toast that is more an "excuse for the glass" than an expression of anything else.*

Starting with the full version of Sheridan's toast, here is a collection of excuses dedicated to such concerns as fleas and riotous monks.

Here's to the maiden of bashful fifteen;
   Here's to the widow of fifty;
Here's to the flaunting extravagant queen,
   And here's to the housewife that's thrifty.
      Let the toast pass—
      Drink to the lass—
I'll warrant she'll prove an excuse for the glass.

Here's to the charmer whose dimples we prize;
   Now to the maid who has none, sir;
Here's to the girl with a pair of blue eyes,
   And here's to the nymph with but one, sir.
      Let the toast pass—
      Drink to the lass—
I'll warrant she'll prove an excuse for the glass.

Here's to the maid with a bosom of snow;
   Now to her that's as brown as a berry;
Here's to the wife with a face full of woe,
   And now for the damsel that's merry.
      Let the toast pass—
      Drink to the lass—
I'll warrant she'll prove an excuse for the glass.

For let 'em be clumsy, or let 'em be slim,
   Young or ancient, I care not a feather:
So fill a pint bumper quite up to the brim,
   And let us e'en toast 'em together.
     Let the toast pass—
     Drink to the lass—
I'll warrant she'll prove an excuse for the glass.

—RICHARD B. SHERIDAN, The School
for Scandal, *Act III*

Great fleas have lesser fleas,
   And these have less to bite 'em;
These fleas have lesser fleas,
   And so *ad infinitum.*
The great fleas themselves in turn,
   Have greater fleas to go on.
While these again have greater still,
   And greater still, and so on.

Here's to the bee—the busy soul;
He has no time for birth control.
That's why it is, in times like these,
We have so many sons of bees!

Here's to the happy, bounding flea:
You cannot tell the he from the she,
But he can tell, and so can she!

—ROLAND YOUNG

I used to know a clever toast,
   But pshaw! I cannot think it—
So fill your glass to anything
   And, bless your souls, I'll drink it.

May riotous monks have a double Lent.

May the skin of your bum never cover a drum.

May we never put our finger in another man's pie.

Shee's pretty to walke with:
And witty to talke with;
And pleasant too to think on.
But the best use of all
Is, her health is a stawle,
And helps us to make us drinke on.

—SIR JOHN SUCKLING

There's many a toast I'd like to say,
If I could only think it;
So fill your glass to anything,
And thank the Lord, I'll drink it!

—WALLACE IRWIN

SEE ALSO: *Bulls; Limericks; Tongue Twisters; World's Worst Toasts*

*For some unexplained reason, relatively large numbers of fishing toasts
exist while other sports and pastimes have inspired few of them. (For
what it is worth, fishing also inspired one of the great provincial newspaper headlines of all time, which appeared in Lenox, Massachusetts, on
January 6, 1933: PRESIDENT COOLIDGE DEAD—MAY HAVE FISHED HERE.)*

A bad day of fishing is still better than a good day at work.

—*Bumper sticker*

A fisherman, 'twixt you and I
Will very seldom tell a lie—
Except when it is needed to
Describe the fish that left his view.

Behold the fisherman!
He riseth in the early morning
And disturbeth the whole household.

Enjoy thy stream, O harmless fish,
And when an angler for his dish,
    Through gluttony's vile sin,
Attempts, the wretch, to pull thee out,
God give thee strength, O gentle trout,
    To pull the rascal in.

Fishing is the chance to wash one's soul
with pure air. It brings meekness
and inspiration, reduces our egotism,
soothes our troubles and shames our wickedness.

—HERBERT HOOVER, *quoted in the*
New York Herald Tribune, *May 19, 1947*

Health to men,
And death to fish;
They're wagging the tails
That will pay for this.

Here's to Fishing—a grand delusion enthusiastically promoted
by glorious liars in old clothes.

—DON MARQUIS

Here's to the fish that I may catch;
So large that even I,
When talking of it afterward,
Will never need to lie.

Here's to our fisherman bold,
Here's to the fish he caught;
Here's to the one that got away,
And here's to the one he bought.

May the holes in your net be no bigger than your fish.

—*Irish*

On an Assyrian tablet of 2000 B.C. we find the following:
"The gods do not subtract from the allotted span of men's
lives the hours spent in fishing."

—HERBERT HOOVER

Rod and line: May they never part company.

Simon Peter saith unto them, I go afishing; they say unto
him, we also go with thee.

—*John 21:3*

The joy of fishing—is fishing.

—HARLAN H. BALLARD

The steady fisherman—who never "reels home."

There are more fish taken out of a stream than ever were
in it.

—OLIVER HERFORD

To the fish—a creature that goes on vacation at about the same time most fishermen do.

A full belly, a heavy purse, and a light heart.

According to the Spanish proverb, four persons are wanted to make a good salad; a spendthrift for oil, a miser for vinegar, a counsellor for salt, and a madman to stir all up.

—ABRAHAM HAYWARD, The Art of Dining

All human history attests
That happiness to man—the hungry sinner—
Since Eve ate apples, much depends on dinner!

—LORD BYRON

Better is a dinner of herbs where love is, than a fatted ox and hatred.

—*Ancient proverb*

Eat, drink and be merry for tomorrow you diet.

Eat well's drink well's brother.

—*Old Scottish proverb*

Good pies and strong beer.

—Poor Robin's Almanack, *1695*

Health to our bodies, peace to our minds, and plenty to our boards.

—Eighteenth-century toast before dinner

I'd rather have a dinner while I'm living than a monument when I'm dead, for the dinner will be on my friends, while the monument would be on me.

"I was always religiously inclined,"
Said the oyster as he slid down
The minister's throat, "but ne'er
Did I dream I'd enter the clergy."

Let the dogs wait a long time.

—Irish wish for a lengthy and ample dinner

May they have sugar to their strawberries!

*—LEIGH HUNT, translated from an
unidentified Italian poet, 1840*

May you always have red-eye gravy with your ham, hush puppies with your catfish, and the good sense not to argue with your wife.

*—Toast from Tennessee, quoted by Timothy
Noah in the* New Republic

O hour of all hours, the most blessed upon earth, the blessed hour of our dinners!

—EDWARD GEORGE LYTTON

On the table spread the cloth,
  Let the knives be sharp and clean;
Pickles get and salad both,
  Let them each be fresh and green.

Only the truly mad eat alone, like Howard Hughes and
Stalin.

—GUY DAVENPORT

With small beer, good ale and wine,
O ye gods! how I shall dine!

Serenely full, the epicure would say,
Fate cannot harm me, I have dined today.

To eat, to drink, and to be merry.

—*Ecclesiastes 8:15*

To Gasteria, the tenth Muse, who presides over the
enjoyments of Taste.

—ANTHELME BRILLAT-SAVARIN

To Mom's cooking:
May my wife never find out how bad it really was.

To soup: May it be seen and not heard.

Unquiet meals make ill digestions.

—SHAKESPEARE,
The Comedy of Errors, *Act V*

We may live without poetry, music and art;
We may live without conscience, and live without heart;
We may live without friends; we may live without books;
But civilized man cannot live without cooks.
We may live without books—what is knowledge but grieving?
We may live without hope—what is hope but deceiving?
We may live without love—what is passion but pining?
But where is the man that can live without dining?

—OWEN MEREDITH *in "Lucile"*

Who can believe with common sense,
A bacon slice gives God offence?
Or how a herring hath a charm
Almighty vengeance to disarm?
Wrapt up in majesty divine,
Does he regard on what we dine?

—JONATHAN SWIFT

SEE ALSO: *Cheeses; Graces; Professional and Occupational (Cooking)*

A day for toil, an hour for sport,
But for a friend life is too short.

—RALPH WALDO EMERSON

A health to you,
A wealth to you,
And the best that life can give to you.
May fortune still be kind to you.
And happiness be true to you,
And life be long and good to you,
Is the toast of all your friends to you.

Absent friends—though out of sight we recognize them with our glasses.

Don't walk in front of me,
   I may not follow.
Don't walk behind me,
   I may not lead.
Walk beside me,
   And just be my friend.

—Irish

Friendship: May differences of opinion cement it.

Friendship's the wine of life.
Let's drink of it and to it.

Here's all that's fine to you!
Books and old wine to you!
Girls be divine to you!

—RICHARD HOVEY

Here's to a friend. He knows you well and likes you just the same.

Here's to beefsteak when you're hungry,
Whiskey when you are dry,
Greenbacks when you are busted,
And Heaven when you die!

Here's to cold nights, warm friends, and a good drink to give them.

Here's to Eternity—may we spend it in as good company as this night finds us.

Here's to our friendship;
May it be reckoned
Long as a lifetime,
Close as a second.

Here's to our friends . . . and the strength to put up with them.

—Line used in ads for the movie The Four Seasons

Here's to the four hinges of Friendship—
Swearing, Lying, Stealing, and Drinking.
When you swear, swear by your country;
When you lie, lie for a pretty woman;
When you steal, steal away from bad company;
And when you drink, drink with me.

Here's to you, old friend, may you live a thousand years,
Just to sort of cheer things in this vale of human tears;
And may I live a thousand too—a thousand—less a day,
'Cause I wouldn't care to be on earth and hear you'd passed away.

It is around the table that friends understand best the warmth of being together.

—Old Italian saying

. . .

I've traveled many a highway
I've walked for many a mile
Here's to the people who made my day
To the people who waved and smiled.

—TOM T. HALL *from* A Gentleman's
Guide to Toasting

May the friends of our youth be the companions of our old age.

May the hinges of friendship never rust, nor the wings of love lose a feather.

—DEAN RAMSAY, *in* Reminiscences of
Scottish Life

May we have more and more friends, and need them less and less!

May we never have friends who, like shadows, follow us in sunshine only to desert us on a cloudy day.

May your tobacco never run out, your library never turn musty, your cellar never go dry, and your friends never turn foes.

More friends and less need of them.

Never drink anything without first smelling it,
Never sign anything without first reading it.
Never dive into pools of depth unknown,
And rarely drink—if you are alone.

—*Seventeenth-century philosophy*

My boat is on the shore,
   And my bark is on the sea;
But, before I go, Tom Moore,
   Here's a double health to thee.

—LORD BYRON, To Thomas Moore

Now I, friend, drink to you, friend,
   As my friend drank to me,
And I, friend, charge you, friend,
   As my friend charged me,
That you, friend, drink to your friend,
   As my friend drank to me;
And the more we drink together, friend,
   The merrier we'll be!

Old friends are scarce,
New friends are few;
Here's hoping I've found
One of each in you.

Pour deep the rosy wine and drink a toast with me;
Here's to three: Thee, Wine, and Camaraderie!

—TOM MOORE

The Lord gives our relatives,
Thank God we can choose our friends.

The world is gay and colorful,
And life itself is new.
And I am very grateful for
The Friend I found in you.

Then here's to thee, old friend; and long
    May thou and I thus meet,
To brighten still with wine and song
    This short life ere it fleet.

To friends: as long as we are able
To lift our glasses from the table.

To my friend. If we ever disagree, may you be in the right.

To our best friends, who know the worst about us
but refuse to believe it.

To the spirit of Christmases yet to come.

—*World War II toast*

We'll think of all the friends we know
And drink to all worth drinking to.

We'll drink the wanting into wealth,
And those that languish into health,
The afflicted into joy, the oppressed
Into serenity and rest.

—CHARLES COTTON

Were't the last drop in the well,
    As I gasp'd upon the brink,
Ere my fainting spirit fell,
    'Tis to thee I would drink.

SEE ALSO: *Alliterative; Biblical; General; Guests; Host/Hostesses; Love; Old Things; Parting*

general

A handsome new nose to you.

A little health, a little wealth,
  A little house and freedom:
With some few friends for certain ends
  But little cause to need 'em.

A toast to the wise
  And a toast to the foolish
A toast to your eyes—
  May they never grow mulish!

A*d multos annos*—to many years!

—*Latin toast from Governor Mario Cuomo
to President Ronald Reagan at the 1988
Gridiron dinner, Washington, D.C.*

All that gives you pleasure.

All true hearts and sound bottoms.

And fill them high with generous juice,
As generous as your mind,
And pledge me in the generous toast—
The whole of human kind!

—ROBERT BURNS

Be glad of life!
Because it gives you the chance to love and work,
To play and to look up at the stars.

—HENRY VAN DYKE

Be not concerned if thou findest thyself in possession of unexpected wealth. Allah will provide an unexpected use for it.

—JAMES JEFFREY ROCHE

Blue skies and green lights.

Call frequently,
Drink moderately,
Park friendly,
Pay today, trust tomorrow.

Days of Ease and Nights of Pleasure.

Delicious nights to every virtuous heart.

Good company, good wine, good welcome make good people.

—SHAKESPEARE

Good day, good health, good cheer, good night!

Health to my body, wealth to my purse,
Heaven to my soul, and I wish you no worse.

Heaven give thee many, many merry days.

—SHAKESPEARE

Here's a toast to all who are here,
No matter where you're from;
May the best day you have seen
Be worse than your worst to come.

Here's hoping how and hoping who
    And hoping when and where;
And may all good things come to you
    Before you cease to care.

Here's to all of us.

—SIR THOMAS LIPTON

Here's to beauty, wit, and wine, and to a full stomach, a full
purse, and a light heart.

Here's to the 'ealth o' your Royal 'ighness; hand my the skin
o' ha gooseberry be big enough for han humbrella to cover up
hall your enemies.

—CADDY's toast in "Erminie"

Here's to us that are here, to you that are there, and the rest
of us everywhere.

—RUDYARD KIPLING

Here's to your good health,
and your family's good health,
and may you all live long and prosper.

—JOSEPH JEFFERSON, actor, as Rip Van Winkle

Here's tow'ds yer an' tew yer!
'F I never had met yet
I'd never hev knewed yer.

I drink to the days that are.

—WILLIAM MORRIS

I wish thee health,
I wish thee wealth,
I wish thee gold in store,
I wish thee heaven upon earth—
What could I wish thee more?

In the garden of life, may your pea pods never be empty.

—BILL COPELAND in Sarasota, Florida,
Journal, quoted in Reader's Digest, June 1982

It is best to rise from life as from the banquet, neither thirsty
nor drunken.

—ARISTOTLE

Love to one, friendship to many, and good will to all.

Make every day a masterpiece.

May life last as long as it is worth wearing.

Make the most of life while you may,
Life is short and wears away!

—WILLIAM OLDYS

May those who deceive us be always deceived.

May our faults be written on the seashore, and every good action prove a wave to wash them out.

May our feast days be many and our fast days be few.

—MARY L. BOOTH

May the clouds in your life form only a background for a lovely sunset.

May the most you wish for be the least you get.

May you have warmth in your igloo, oil in your lamp, and peace in your heart.

—*Eskimo toast*

May we all live in pleasure and die out of debt.

May we be happy and our enemies know it.

May we live respected and die regretted.

May we breakfast with Health, dine with Friendship, crack a bottle with Mirth, and sup with the goddess Contentment.

May we live to learn well,
And learn to live well.

May we never do worse.

May we never feel want, nor ever want feeling.

May we never flatter our superiors or insult our inferiors.

May we never know want till relief is at hand.

May you always distinguish between the weeds and the flowers.

May you be merry and lack nothing.

—SHAKESPEARE

May you get it all together before you come apart.

—BILL LEARY, *quoted in* Reader's Digest,
June 1982

May you have the hindsight to know where you've been. . . .
The foresight to know where you're going.

—CHARLES M. MEYERS

May you live all the days of your life.

—JONATHAN SWIFT

May you live as long as you want to and want to as long as you live.

May your life be as beautiful as a summer day with just enough clouds to make you appreciate the sunshine.

—*Found inscribed in a book and dated 1882*

So live that when you come to die, even the undertaker will feel sorry for you.

—MARK TWAIN

Success to the lover, honor to the brave,
Health to the sick, and freedom to the slave.

The riotous enjoyment of a quiet conscience.

The three generals in power: General Employment, General Industry, and General Comfort.

There is no satiety
In our society
With the variety
of your *esprit*.
Here's a long purse to you,
And a great thirst to you!
Fate be no worse to you
Than she's been to me!

'Tis hard to tell which is best,
Music, Food, Drink, or Rest.

'Tis not so bad a world,
As some would like to make it;
But whether good or whether bad,
Depends on how you take it.

To the old, long life and treasure;
To the young, all health and pleasure;
   To the fair, their face,
   With eternal grace;
And the rest, to be loved at leisure.

—BEN JONSON

Two ins and one out—in health, wealth, and out of debt.

While we live, let us live.

Wit without virulence, wine without excess, and wisdom
without affectation.

You shall and you shan't,
  You will and you won't,
You're condemned if you do,
  And you are damned if you don't.

Be present at our table, Lord.
Be here and everywhere adored.
These mercies bless, and grant that we
May feast in Paradise with Thee.

—JOHN CENNICK, 1741

Bless, O Lord, this food to our use, and us to Thy service,
and make us ever needful of the needs of others, in Jesus'
name, Amen.

—*Traditional Protestant grace*

Bless this food and us that eats it.

—*Cowboy grace*

Bless us, O Lord, and these Thy gifts which we have received
out of Thy bounty, through Christ Our Lord. Amen.

—*Traditional Catholic grace*

Come, Lord Jesus, Be our Guest, and let Thy gifts to us be
blessed. Amen.

For a' Thou'st placed upon the table, we thank the Lord, as well's we're able.

For the air we breathe,
and the water we drink,
For a soul and a mind
with which to think,
For food that comes
from fertile sod,
For these, and many things
I'm thankful to my God.

—Thanksgiving Grace written by comedian
Danny Thomas when he was in the sixth grade.

For rabbits young and rabbits old,
For rabbits hot, and rabbits cold,
For rabbits tender, rabbits tough,
We thank Thee, Lord, we've had enough!

—DEAN SWIFT, who undoubtedly suffered
from an endless round of luncheons in his
honor, just as today's celebrities do. But
whereas the modern complaint might be of too
much chicken, Swift had a different lament.

For what we are about to receive, the Lord make us truly thankful, for Christ's sake. Amen.

—Old English classic which is probably the
best known of all Christian English-language graces.

God bless the master of this house,
God bless the mistress too;
And all the little children
Who round the table go.

—Traditional British grace

God is great, God is good,
We will thank Him for this food.
By his hand must all be fed
Thanks be to God for our daily bread.

—Traditional children's grace

Good bread, good meat
Good God, let's eat!

Heavenly father bless us,
And keep us all alive;
There's ten of us for dinner
And not enough for five.

Give me a good digestion, Lord,
    And also something to digest;
Give me a healthy body, Lord,
    And sense to keep it at its best.

—DR. FURSE, bishop of St. Albans

Lift up your hands toward the sanctuary and bless the Lord.
Blessed art Thou, O Lord our God, King of the Universe,
who brings forth bread from the earth. Amen.

—Traditional Jewish thanksgiving before meals

May the Lord make us thankful for what we are about to
receive, and for what Mr. Jones hath already received. Amen.

> *—Grace used to rebuke anyone who starts*
> *eating too soon.*

May the good Lord take a liking to you—but not too soon!

May the holy Saints be about your bed, and about your
board, from this time to the latter end—God help us all!

> *—Irish*

O Lord above, send us thy grace
   to be our stay,
So as we never do that which brings
   unto the wicked sinful way,
The wicked sinful way.

> *—THOMAS WYTHORNE. This grace was*
> *sung and is believed to be one used by the*
> *Pilgrims on the Mayflower.*

O thou that blest the loaves and fishes,
Look down upon these two poor dishes,
And tho' the murphies* are but small,
O make them large enough for all,
For if they do our bellies fill
I'm sure it is a miracle.

Praise to God who giveth meat,
Convenient unto all to eat;
Praise for tea and buttered toast,
Father, Son, and Holy Ghost.

> *—Old Scottish grace*

* Murphies are potatoes.

Some have meat but cannot eat;
Some could eat but have no meat;
We have meat and can all eat;
Blest, therefore, be God for our meat.

—The Selkirk Grace *found in the papers
of Dr. Plume of Maldon, Essex, in a
handwriting of about 1650.*

Another version, attributed to Robert Burns:

Some hae meat, and canna eat,
  And some wad eat that want it;
But we hae meat, and we can eat,
  And sae the Lord be thankit.

Thank the Lord for what we've gotten,
If ther 'ad been mooar, mooar we shud hev etten.

What we are about to receive, may the Trinity and Unity
bless, Amen.

—*Grace before meat*

For thy benefits, O Lord, we give Thee thanks.

—*Grace after meat*

guests

Here's to our guest—
Don't let him rest.
But keep his elbow bending.
'Tis time to drink—
Full time to think
Tomorrow—when you're mending.

May our house always be too small to hold all our friends.

—MYRTLE REED

Our house is ever at your service.

See, your guests approach:
Address yourself to entertain them sprightly,
And let's be red with mirth.

—SHAKESPEARE, Winter's Tale, *Act IV*

Stay happy, my friend, hang easy and loose
Gettin' rattlesnake-riled is just no use
So here is a slogan that's sure hard to match
There ain't no use itchin' unless you can scratch!

—*Cowboy welcome from a sampler*

The ornament of a house is the guests who frequent it.

To Our Guest! A friend of our friend's is doubly our friend.
Here's to him.

You are welcome here
Be at your ease
Get up when ready
Go to bed when you please.
Happy to share with you
Such as we've got
The leaks in the roof
The soup in the pot.
You don't have to thank us

Or laugh at our jokes
Sit deep and come often
You're one of the folks.

> —*Notice found in Aspen, Colorado, guest
> house and quoted by Erica Wilson in the
> Washington Post, 1980.*

SEE ALSO: *Friendship; General; Hosts/Hostesses; Parting*

*Early to rise and early to bed
makes a male healthy and wealthy
and dead.*

—JAMES THURBER

Here's a health to every one;
Peace on earth, and heaven won.

Here's to your health—a long life and an easy death to you.

Here's to your health! You make age curious, Time furious,
and all of us envious.

That a doctor might never earn a dollar out of you
And that your heart may never give out.

The best doctors in the world are Doctor Diet, Doctor Quiet,
and Dr. Merryman.

—JONATHAN SWIFT

The health of the salmon to you: a long life,
a full heart and a wet mouth!

—*Irish*

To your good health, old friend,
may you live for a thousand years,
and I be there to count them.

—ROBERT SMITH SURTEES

SEE ALSO: *Alliterative; Friendship; General*

hell &
damnation

Here's to Hell!
May the stay there
Be as much fun as the way there!

Here's to Mephisto! Goodness knows
What we would do without him.
And, good Mephisto, do not spurn
Our toast with mocking laughter;
Nor yet the compliment return
But toasting us hereafter.

—OLIVER HEREFORD

Here's to the Pavement of Hell,
And the tiresome old teachers who talk it.
Observation has taught
That we shall not be caught
Entirely alone, when we walk it.

Here's to those who love us well—
Those who don't may go to Hell.

—JAMES KEENE

Here's to you
Here's to me
May we never disagree.
But, if we do,
to Hell with you—
and here's to me!

Up friends, up!
   Tonight we sup,
Though tomorrow we die of revel!
   Rise for a toast,
   Though tomorrow we roast;
A Health to His Lordship, the Devil!

SEE ALSO: *Curses*

Hints for Effective Toasting

・ ・ ・

1. *Do it in a way that is most comfortable to you. You may remain seated.* Legend has it that it became acceptable to toast without standing in Britain during the reign of Charles II. The king allowed that this would be acceptable after he had risen in response to a toast in his honor while aboard the ship *Royal Charles* and bashed his head into a beam. A similar bashing to King William IV, when he was heir to the throne and toasted George IV while aboard a man-of-war, forever ended the custom of standing toasts in the Royal Navy.

2. *Don't mix toasts with other messages.* During World War II at a banquet given by Marshal Joseph Stalin at the Russian embassy in Teheran, Stalin rose to his feet after Churchill, Roosevelt, and other leaders had been toasted. He grinned and made a quick, impromptu remark in Russian. Judging from the smiles on the faces of the Russians present, it could only be concluded that he had come up with a witty and appropriate toast. As the Americans and British grabbed their glasses, the interpreter rose to say, "Marshal Stalin says the men's room is on the right."

3. *If you are in some position where you are likely to be called on, it is a good idea to have a few short toasts memorized.* A groom at his own wedding banquet was asked to propose a toast to the bride. Unprepared, he got to his feet, put his hand on the bride's shoulder and said, "Ladies and gentlemen, I . . . I don't know what to say. This thing was forced upon me—"

4. *Check the context of your toast if it is quoted from a known poem or prose work.* Prince Philip of Great Britain was told the story of the man who toasted him at a banquet with two lines from John Dryden:

・ ・ ・

A man so various he seemed to be
Not one but all mankind's epitome.

Philip liked the lines and later looked up the remaining lines of the poem:

Stiff in opinions, always in the wrong
Was everything but starts and nothing long;
But in the course of revolving moon
Was chemist, fiddler, statesman and buffoon.

5. *Don't get ahead of yourself.* When Queen Louise of Prussia met the conquering Napoleon she drank to him: "To the health and kindness of Napoleon the Great. He has taken our states, and soon will return them to us." Napoleon bowed and replied, "Do not drink it all, Madame."

6. *Make sure that the toast you are delivering is appropriate to the group at hand.* "Bottoms up" would be inappropriate at the beginning of a boat race.

7. *Don't push somebody who is not so inclined to propose a toast. The result may not be the one desired.* There are many examples but a perfect case in point involved Winston Churchill in the 1920s after he had served as First Lord of the Admiralty. At a dinner party, someone pestered him for a toast to the traditions of the Royal Navy. "The traditions of the Royal Navy?" was his final response, "I'll give you the traditions of the Royal Navy. Rum, buggery and the lash."

8. *When proposing a toast, make sure you know what you are drinking.* Basic advice, but listen to Rudy Maxa reporting on toasting in the nation's capital in the September 1986 *Washingtonian:* "Then there's the story, perhaps apocryphal, about an American military man toasting his Jap-

anese hosts at a Washington dinner party. Mistaking a finger bowl for a goblet, he finished his remarks and drank deeply from the bowl. Not wishing to offend, fellow guests reached for their own finger bowls and followed suit."

9. *Don't drink with old Saxons.* An Old Saxon toasting custom required that a man draw the sharp edge of his knife across his forehead, letting the blood drip into his wine cup and then drinking a health to the woman he loved.

SEE ALSO: *Secrets; Toastmaster*

What follows is a small, chronologically displayed museum of special toasts that were tied to a historic place, cause, or event. There have been hundreds more, but these were some of the most important. One should also be aware of the fact that any number of mottos and rallying cries— "Fifty-four Forty or Fight!" "Remember the Alamo!" "Remember the Maine!" "Keep 'em flying!"—were also toasts in their time.

Love and wine are the bonds that fasten us all,
The world but for these to confusion would fall,
Were it not for the pleasures of love and good wine,
Mankind, for each trifle their lives would resign;
They'd not value dull life nor could live without thinking,
Nor would kings rule the world but for love and good
    drinking.

—Toast of 1675

Mr. Payne, to err is nature; to rectify error is glory. I believe
I was wrong yesterday.

—GEORGE WASHINGTON, 1754, *after*
an argument with a man named William Payne.
It had been expected that Washington might
challenge the man to a duel. Instead he sent
Payne wine and the toast to drink it with.

Some delight in fighting Fields,
Nobler transports Bacchus yields,
Fill the bowl I ever said,
'Tis better to lie drunk than dead."

—*Toast of 1766*

And he that will this health deny,
Down among the dead men let him lie.

—JOHN DYER, *from his "Here's a Health to*
the King," eighteenth century

Here's to the squire who goes on parade,
Here's to the citizen soldier.
Here's to the merchant who fights for his trade,
Whom danger increasingly makes bolder,
  Let mirth appear,
  Every heart cheer,
The toast that I give is to the brave volunteer.

—*American Revolution*

Freedom from mobs as well as kings.

—*American, late eighteenth century*

We mutually pledge to each other our lives, our fortunes,
and our sacred honor.

—THOMAS JEFFERSON

When lifting high the rosy glass,
Each comrade toasts his favorite lass
And to his fond bosom near;
Ah, how can I the nectar sip,
Or Anna's name escape my lip
When Mary is my dear?

—Sailor's toast, 1795

Stand to your glasses steady,
  And drink to your comrade's eyes:
Here's a cup to the dead already,
  And hurrah for the next that dies.

*—Refrain from a long, morose toast with much lore
attached to it. Depending on your source,
it was a hymn to cholera, the toast of the English
dying in the Black Hole of Calcutta in 1758,
or a pledge of soldiers during the first Burmese
war. It has been attributed to several
authors including Alfred Domett and Bartholomew
Dowling. During World War I it was used by
British and American pilots.*

Ladies and Gentlemen, this is the last time I shall drink to
your health as a public man. I do it with all sincerity, wishing
you all possible happiness.

*—GEORGE WASHINGTON. On March 3, 1797,
the day before he retired from office, he gave
a dinner for President-elect John Adams
at which he raised his glass and gave this toast.*

Rum—the greatest undertaker upon earth.

*—Early American temperance toast (to be
drunk in water)*

Ask nothing that is not clearly right, and submit to nothing that is wrong.

—ANDREW JACKSON'S *motto, often used as a toast in the nineteenth century.*

Another toast attributed to Jackson went like this:

"Here's to an honest man—the noblest work of God."

May we never have a Fox too cunning nor a Pitt too deep.

—*English, early nineteenth century. It refers to Charles James Fox and William Pitt, the two great political figures.*

To the total abolition of the slave trade.

—*Abolitionist's toast*

May the blackness of heart, not blackness of face, distinguish the free man from the slave.

—*Early abolitionist sentiment. Appeared first in England in 1812 but was soon embraced by Americans who opposed slavery.*

Up to my lips and down to my hips
The further it goes, the better it gits
Here's peace at home and plenty abroad—
Love your wife and serve the Lord—Drink!

—*Toast of the antebellum South*

Here's to ye, Mr. Lincoln! May you die both late and aisy,
And when you lie with the top of each toe turned up to the
   roots of the daisy,
May this be your epitaph nately writ:
"Tho' traitors abused him vilely,
He was honest and koind, and loved a joke,
And he pardoned Miles O'Reilley."

—MILES O'REILLEY, *pseudonym of Charles
Graham Halpine, from* Life and
Adventures, *etc., of Private Miles O'Reilly*

I *drink to all, whate'er their creed,*
   Their country, rank, communion,
Who in the cause of Freedom bleed,
   And combat for the Union!

—*Union toast*

There are bonds of all sorts in this world of ours,
   Letters of friendship and ties of flowers,
   And true lovers' knots I ween;
The girl and boy and bound by a kiss,
But there's never a bond, old friend like this:
   We have drunk from the same canteen!

—GEN. CHARLES G. HALPINE. *This toast
was very popular among the Union veterans
of the Grand Army of the Republic.*

Under the sod and the dew,
   Waiting the judgment day;
Love and tears for the blue,
   Tears and love for the gray.

—FRANCIS M. FINCH

Nine times nine cheers!

—*Nineteenth-century English toast often
directed at Queen Victoria. Over time, it
became shortened to "Cheers!"*

May the New Year grant you
a clean shirt
a clear conscience
and a ticket to California in your pocket.

—*Irish, nineteenth century*

To the memory of
GEORGE WASHINGTON
The childless father of seventy millions.

—*Popular nineteenth-century toast*

Solitary and alone in its grandeur stands forth the character
of Washington in history: solitary and alone like some peak
that has no fellow in the mountain range of greatness.

—SENATOR JOHN W. DANIELS, *of Virginia,
at the dedication of Washington's Monument*

Huge and alert, irascible yet strong,
We make our fitful way 'mid right and wrong.
One time we pour out millions to be free,
Then rashly sweep an empire from the sea!
One time we strike the shackles from the slaves,
And then, quiescent, we are ruled by knaves.
Often we rudely break restraining bars,
And confidently reach out toward the stars.

Yet under all there flows a hidden stream
Sprung from the Rock of Freedom, the great dream
Of Washington and Franklin, men of old
Who knew that freedom is not bought with gold.

This is the Land we love, our heritage,
Strange mixture of the gross and fine, yet sage.
And full of promise—destined to be great
Drink to Our Native Land! God Bless the State!

—ROBERT BRIDGES, *"A Toast to Our*
Native Land," late nineteenth century

To our country: May her literary men do her honor by
speaking the truth, of her and all things; may they give her
immortality by making the truth eloquent and beautiful.

—WOODROW WILSON, *as president of*
Princeton, to Lucy Smith of New Orleans in
a letter of December 8, 1898

A mighty nation mourns thee yet;
Thy gallant crew—their awful fate;
And justice points her finger straight,
Lest we forget—lest we forget!

—*On the sinking of the* Maine

Home, boys, home! It's home we ought to be!
Home, boys, home! In God's country;
Where the ash and the oak and weeping willow tree
And the grass grows green in North Ameriky!

—*Toast of the U.S. Army in the Philippines*
at the end of the Spanish-American War

Their arms our sure defense,
Our arms, their recompense,
    Fall in!

—*Women's toast to men returning from the*
Spanish-American War

May it always carry messages of happiness.

—*On the christening of the Honolulu cable*
between San Francisco and Hawaii,
December 15, 1902

Here's to the Trusts which are not dead as yet,
For the longer you curse 'em the stronger they get.
So if we would strangle their dragon-like breath
Let's try a new method and bless 'em to death.

—WALLACE IRWIN, 1904

To all who put their trust in God—but never their God in a
Trust.

Gentlemen, I believe your victories were won on water.

—WILLIAM JENNINGS BRYAN *asked to*
toast the British navy, which he did with a
glass of water.

A glass of good Nature's ale—may its recipe never fail.

—*Water toast of the antisaloon forces, early*
twentieth century. "Nature's Ale," of course,
refers to water, as does the synonymous
"Adam's Ale."

Ireland—St. Patrick destroyed its creeping things of other
days—may his disciples speedily exterminate the political
reptiles of the present age.

—*Irish, early twentieth century*

I've burnt the midnight oil, many knotty problems solving;
I've ponder'd o'er human woes, including those involving
The rights of lovely women, to which they cling like leeches;
But, tell me, (for I'm all at sea,
As to what the moral teaches)—
When the dears go out to vote, are they to wear our breeches?

—PAUL LOWE, *antisuffragette toast, 1910*

See our glorious banner waving,
  Hear the bugle call;
Rally comrades to the standard
  Down with alcohol!

—*American nonalcoholic toast, popular*
among temperance groups, circa 1915

To our women, our horses, and the men who ride them.

—*Calvary toast, World War I, from the French*

To the automobile; the rich man's wine and the poor man's chaser.

Here's to my car and your car, and may they never meet.

To the confounding of our enemies.

—*Toast favored and made popular by Dean Acheson*

Here's to today!
For tomorrow we may be radioactive.

—*Early Atomic Age toast*

Every president seeks to use the press. The press can take care of itself and hopefully so can a president. I hope that my epitaph will be with relations to the White House press corps, "He gave as good as he got."

—RONALD REAGAN, *making his farewell to the White House Press corps, April 21, 1988*

I would like to propose a toast to a future of peace for the Soviet and the American people and for all nations on earth, to idealism and idealists, to the health of the president of the United States of America, Mr. George Bush, and Barbara Bush, to the health and well-being of all present here, to the happiness of our children and grandchildren.

—*Historic toast proposed by President Gorbachev, on June 1, 1990, at the Russian embassy during the summit in Washington.*

George Bush's response:

Ladies and gentlemen, I invite all of you to join me in a toast to our gracious hosts, President and Mrs. Gorbachev, to lasting peace, and to this wonderful spirit of freedom.

SEE ALSO: *Alliterative; America; Military; Prohibition; Secrets; Temperant*

God bless our mortgaged home.

Here's to home, the place where we are treated best, and grumble the most.

—*From an old postcard*

Long may your lum reek.

—ROBERT BURNS (*Translation: "Long
may your chimney smoke"*)

May blessings be upon your house,
   Your roof and hearth and walls;
May there be lights to welcome you
   When evening's shadow falls—
The love that like a guiding star
   Still signals when you roam;
A book, a friend—these be the things
   That make a house a home.

—MYRTLE REED, *a house blessing*

SEE ALSO: *General; Guests; Hosts/Hostesses*

hosts & hostesses

A toast to our host
   And a song from the short and tall of us,
May he live to be
   The guest of all of us!

Here's a health to thine and thee,
   not forgetting mine and me.
When thine and thee again meet mine and me,
may mine and me have as much welcome for thine and thee
as thine and thee have had for mine and me tonight.

—*Irish*

Here's to our hostess, considerate and sweet;
Her wit is endless, but when do we eat?

I thank you for your welcome which was cordial,
And your cordial, which is welcome.

Let's drink to the maker of the feast, our friend and host.
May his generous heart, like his good wine, only grow
mellower with the years.

May the roof above us never fall in, and may we friends
gathered below never fall out.

—Irish

May you be Hung, Drawn and Quartered!
Yes—Hung with diamonds,
Drawn in a coach and four,
And quartered in the best houses in the land.

To our host,
An excellent man;
For is not a man
Fairly judged by the
Company he keeps?

To the sun that warmed the vineyard,
   To the juice that turned to wine,
To the host that cracked the bottle,
   And made it yours and mine.

To our hostess! She's a gem. We love her, God bless her.
And the devil take her husband.

110

To our host: The rapturous, wild, and ineffable pleasure of drinking at somebody else's expense.

—HENRY SAMBROOKE LEIGH, *1870*

What's a table richly spread
Without a woman at its head?

You are welcome, my fair guests; that noble lady,
Our gentleman, that is not freely merry,
Is not my friend: This to confirm my welcome:
And to you all good health.

—SHAKESPEARE, Henry VIII, *Act I*

SEE ALSO: *Friendship; General; Guests*

Here's to the man who loves his wife,
   And loves his wife alone.
For many a man loves another man's wife,
   When he ought to be loving his own.

May your life be long and sunny
And your husband fat and funny.

To my husband—may he never be tight; but tight or sober, my husband.

When the husband drinks to the wife, all would be well; when the wife drinks to the husband, all is.

—*Old English proverb*

SEE ALSO: *Alliterative; Anniversaries; Man/Men; Weddings*

An assembly of short toasts or, as they have been called, cheers to get you through a United Nations reception. Their English equivalents are along the lines of Cheers, To your health, and Bottoms up.

Albanian: Gëzuar.

Arabian: Bismillah. Fi schettak.

Armenian: Genatzt.

Austrian: Prosit.

Belgian: Op uw gezonheid.

Brazilian: Saúde. Viva.

Chinese: Nien Nien nu e. Kong Chien. Kan bei. Yum sen. Wen lie.

Czechoslovakian: Na Zdravi. Nazdar.

Danish: Skål.

Dutch: Proost. Geluch.

Egyptian: Fee sihetak.

Esperanto: Je zia sano.

Estonian: Tervist.

Finnish: Kippis. Maljanne.

French: A votre santé. Santé.

German: Prosit. Auf ihr wohl.

Greek: Eis Igian.

Greenlandic: Kasûgta.

Hawaiian: Okole maluna. Hauoli maoli oe. Meli kalikama.

Hungarian: Kedves egeszsegere.

Icelandic: Santanka nu.

Indian: Jaikind. Aanand.

Indonesian: Selamat.

Iranian: Besalmati. Shemoh.

Italian: A la salute. Salute. Cin cin.

Japanese: Kampai. Banzai.

Korean: Kong gang ul wi ha yo.

Lithuanian: I sveikas.

Malayan: Slamat minum.

Mexican: Salud.

Moroccan: Saha wa'afiab.
New Zealand: Kia ora.
Norwegian: Skål.
Pakistani: Sanda bashi.
Philippine: Mabuhay.
Polish: Na zdrowie. Vivat.
Portuguese: A sua saúde.
Romanian: Noroc. Pentru sanatatea dunneavoastra.
Russian: Na zdorovia.
Spanish: Salud. Salud, amor y pesetas y el tiempo para gustarlos! (Health, love, and money and the time to enjoy them!)
Swedish: Skål.
Thai: Sawasdi.
Turkish: Şerefe.
Ukrainian: Boovatje zdorovi.
Welsh: Iechyd da.
Yugoslavian: Zivio.
Zulu: Oogy wawa.

SEE ALSO: *Irish; Latin; Scotch*

i r i s h

There is no area of the world where English is spoken—and probably none where any other language is spoken for that matter—that can compare to Ireland as a stronghold for the custom of toasting. More often than not, toasts go by the name of "blessings" in Ireland. There are large numbers of them, and their use seems to be on the increase. John B. Keane said in a recent article on the subject, "Nothing has the grace or the beauty of an old Irish blessing and recently I was delighted to learn that instead of dying out, Irish blessings are on the increase. All you have to do is listen and if you spend a day in the Irish countryside you will go away with countless blessings ringing in your ears."

Blessings are often used beyond the reach of a glass, but all make appropriate toasts. A graveside blessing—"That the devil mightn't hear of his death till he's safe inside the walls of heaven"—can be equally appropriate as a toast to the departed.

The vast majority of toasts in this section (along with others scattered throughout the rest of the book) come from the collection of Jack McGowan of the Irish Distillers International of Dublin, who has pulled them together from all over his nation.

One other thing. Many Irish toasts are one-liners that lend themselves to being assembled into longer toasts. This is especially true of the many May you's.

A goose in your garden except on Christmas day.

Health and long life to you.
The wife/husband of your choice to you.
A child every year to you.
Land without rent to you.
And may you be half-an-hour in heaven
before the devil knows you're dead.
Slante! [Pronounced *slawn-cheh;* it means Health!]

Health and long life to you
The wife of your choice to you
Land free of rent to you
From this day forth.

Here's to you, _____. When God measures you, may he put the tape around your big and generous heart and not around your small and foolish head.

May the frost never afflict your spuds.
May the outside leaves of your cabbage always be free from
    worms.
May the crows never pick your haystack and may your
    donkey always be in foal.

May those who love us love us;
And those that don't love us,
May God turn their hearts;
And if He doesn't turn their hearts,
May He turn their ankles,
So we'll know them by their limping.

May you have warm words on a cold evening,
A full moon on a dark night,
And the road downhill all the way to your door.

[*For the bachelor*]

May you have nicer legs than yours under the table before
the new spuds are up.

Health to Everyone
From the tip of the roof to the side of the fire
From wall to wall
And if there's anyone *in* the wall, speak up!

Here's a health to your enemies' enemies!

Here's that ye may never die nor be kilt till ye break your
bones over a bushel of glory.

Here's to a fair price on a fair day.

Here's to eyes in your head and none in your spuds!

Here's to health, peace, and prosperity;
May the flower of love never be nipped by the frost of
disappointment; nor shadow of grief fall among a member of
this circle.

Here's to the land of the shamrock so green,
Here's to each lad and his darling colleen,
Here's to the ones we love dearest and most,
And may God save old Ireland—that's an Irishman's toast.

Here's to your health
May God bring you luck
And may your journey be smooth and happy.

"It's not a sin not to be Irish," says Sean O'Huiginn, former consul general of Ireland, "but it is a great shame."

May meat always sweeten your pot.

May the day keep fine for you.

May the devil say a prayer for you.

May the enemies of Ireland never meet a friend.

May the horns of your cattle touch heaven.

May the path to hell grow green
For lack of travelers.

May the road rise to meet you.
May the wind be always at your back,
the sun shine warm upon your face,
the rain fall soft upon your fields,
and until we meet again
may God hold you in the hollow of His hand.

May the rocks in your field turn to gold.

May the saints protect you,
And sorrow neglect you,
And bad luck to the one
That doesn't respect you.

May the ship that took your sons away
to farm the Californias
bring home a harvest of riches for Christmas.

May the sun shine warm upon your face and the rains
fall soft upon your fields.

May the swallows be first in your eaves.
May your milk never turn.
May your horses never stray.
May your hens always lay.
May lean bacon hang from your rafters.

May the thatch on your house
be as strong as the thatch on your head;
May the moon be as full as your glass and American dollars
arrive in the post by Christmas.

May there always be work for your hands to do.
May your purse always hold a coin or two.
May the sun always shine on your windowpane.
May a rainbow be certain to follow each rain.
May the hand of a friend always be near you.
May God fill your heart with gladness to cheer you.

May time never turn your head gray.

May we all be alive this time in twelve months.

May what goes down not come back up again.

May you always wear silk.

May you be seven times better off a year from now.

May you die in bed at ninety-five years, shot by a jealous husband/wife.

May you have the hindsight to know where you've been, the foresight to know where you're going, and the insight to know when you're going too far.

May you look back on the past with as much pleasure as you look forward to the future.

May you never give cherries to pigs or advice to a fool nor praise the green corn till you've seen the ripe field.

May you never have to eat your hat.

May you never make an enemy
when you could make a friend
unless you meet a fox among your chickens.

May your fire be as warm as the weather is cold.

May your fire never go out.

May your shadow never gross less.

May your well never run dry.

No wasps near your honey, but bees in your hive.

That a doctor might never earn a dollar out of you and that
your heart might never give out.

That the ten toes of your feet might always steer you
clear of misfortune, and I hope,
before you're much older,
that you'll hear much better toasts than this.
  Slante!

The Irish heart—Quick and strong in its generous impulses,
firm in its attachments, sound to the core.

To a full moon on a dark night
And the road downhill all the way to your door.

To a warm bed, a dry stook,* and glass in your window.

To the thirst that is yet to come.

To the three skills of a hare
sharp turning
high jumping
and strong running against the hill.

* A stook is a sheaf of grain.

To twenty years a growing
twenty years at rest
twenty years declining
and twenty years when it doesn't matter
whether we're there or not.

To warm words on a cold day.

Wert thou all that I wish thee,
Great, glorious and free,
First flower of the earth,
And first gem of the sea.

—TOM MOORE

Your Health! May we have one together in ten years time
and a few in between.

SEE ALSO: *Babies/Children; Birthdays; Bulls; Christmas; Death; Food;
Health; Historic; Hosts/Hostesses; New Years; St. Patrick's Day; Weddings*

The prime Jewish toast is the Hebrew L'chayim, *which means "to life,"
or "to your health."* Mazel tov *is also used as a toast. Leo Rosten explains
which to use when in his* Joys of Yiddish: *"Some innocents confuse*
L'chayim *with* mazel tov, *using one when the other would be appropriate. There is no reason to err.* L'chayim *is used whenever one would
say 'Your health,' 'Cheers!' or (I shudder to say) 'Here's mud in your eye.'*
Mazel tov! *is used as 'Congratulations.'"*

Latin

Ad finem esto fidelis. Be faithful to the end.

Amor patriae. The love of our country.

Dilige amicos. Love your friends.

Dum vivimus vivamus. Let us live while we live.

Esto perpetua. Be thou perpetual.

Propino tibi. I drink to you.

Libations

A drink, my lass, in a deep clear glass,
Just properly tempered by ice,
And here's to the lips mine have kissed,
And if they were thine, here's twice.

A glass in the hand's worth two on the shelf—
Tipple it down and refresh yourself!

A small glass and thirsty!
Be sure never ask it:
Man might as well serve up
His soup in a basket.

—LEIGH HUNT

A toast to any gentleman
So shrewd and diplomatic
Who never—though he's in his cups—
Decides he's operatic!

At the punch bowl's brink
Let the thirsty think
   What they say in Japan:
"First the man takes a drink,
Then the drink takes a drink,
   Then the drink takes the man!"

Better to pay the tavernkeeper than the druggist.

                                       —Spanish

Come, friends, come let us drink again,
This liquid from the nectar vine,
For water makes you dumb and stupid,
Learn this from the fishes—
They cannot sing, nor laugh, nor drink
This beaker full of sparkling wine.

                              —Old Dutch song

Drink and be merry, for our time on earth is short, and
death lasts forever.

Drink, for you know not
   When you came, nor why,
Drink, for you know not why
   You go, nor whence.

                            —OMAR KHAYYÁM

Drink today and drown all sorrow,
You shall perhaps not do't tomorrow
Best while you have it, use your breath;
There is no drinking after death.

—FRANCIS BEAUMONT *and*
JOHN FLETCHER, The Blood Brother

Drink with impunity—
Or anyone who happens to invite you!

—ARTEMUS WARD

Fill the bumper fair;
  Every drop we sprinkle
O'er the brow of care,
  Smooths away a wrinkle.

—TOM MOORE

Fill up the goblet, let it swim
In foam, that overlooks the brim;
He that drinks deepest, here's to him.

—CHARLES COTTON

Hath thy ale virtue or thy beer strength, that the tongue of
man may be tickled and his palate pleased in the morning.

—BEN JONSON

He who goes to bed, and goes to bed sober,
Falls as the leaves do, and dies in October;
But he who goes to bed, and does so mellow,
Lives as he ought to, and dies a good fellow.

—*Parody on Beaumont and Fletcher's toast*
from The Blood Brother

Here is a toast to all the toasts,
   As toasted they should be,
Given by paupers, kings, and hosts,
   With much felicity.

It flies o'er mountains, swims the sea,
   Tunnels the earth below,
Spreading conviviality
   Wherever it doth go.

It is not great, nor is it small,
   Is neither far nor near.
A well-considered wish from all,
   "Another bottle here."

—JAMES MONROE MCLEAN,
The Book of Wine

Here's to the temperance supper,
   With water in glasses tall,
And coffee and tea to end with—
   And me not there at all.

Here's to the bottle which holds a store
Of imprisoned joy and laughter!
   Here's to this bottle,
   Many more bottles,
And others to follow after.

Here's to the man who takes the pledge,
Who keeps his word and does not hedge,
Who won't give up and won't give in
Till the last man's out and there's no more gin.

Here's to water, the best of things that man to man can bring.
But who am I, that I should have the best of everything?

Let Princes revel at the pump, let peers with ponds make
    free;
But whiskey, wine, and even beer, is good enough for me.

Here's to you that makes me wear old clothes;
Here's to you that turns my friends to foes,
But seeing you're so near—here goes!
Here it goes under my nose—
God knows I need it.

Here's may we never drink worse!

Ho, gentlemen! Lift your glasses up,
Each gallant, each swain and lover;
A kiss to the beads that brim in the cup,
A laugh for the foam spilt over.

Honor, love, fame, wealth may desert us, but thirst is eternal.

I drink no more than a sponge.

—FRANÇOIS RABELAIS

I drink to your health when I'm with you,
I drink to your health when I'm alone,
I drink to your health so often
I'm beginning to worry about my own.

I drink when I have occasion and sometimes when I have no occasion.

—MIGUEL DE CERVANTES

If all be true as we do think
There are five reasons why we drink:
Good wine, a Friend, or being Dry
Or lest one should be, by and by . . .
Or any other reason why!

—HENRY ALDRICH, dean of Christ
Church, circa 1620

In an honest tavern let me die,
Before my lips a brimmer lie,
And angel choirs come down and cry,
"Peace to thy soul, my jolly boy."

—WALTER DE MAPES

Kings it makes gods, and meaner creatures, kings.

—SHAKESPEARE, King Richard III, Act V

Let schoolmasters puzzle their brain
With grammar and nonsense and learning;
Good liquor, I stoutly maintain,
Gives genius a better discerning.

—OLIVER GOLDSMITH

"Lips that touch liquor shall never touch mine";
Thus cried the maiden with fervor divine;
But from her statement what must we infer—
They shan't touch her liquor, or shan't touch her?

—PUCK in Shakespeare's Midsummer Night's Dream

126

May the beam of the glass never destroy the ray of the mind.

May the bloom of the face never extend to the nose.

May the tears of the tankard afford us relief.

May you ever have lived—
   May you ever have loved—
So that good drink—
   Will never make you think—
You might have done better.

Mingle with the friendly bowl,
The feast of reason and the flow of soul.

—ALEXANDER POPE

Now here's to Addition—
   Another pint, pray!
Then here's to Subtraction—
   Take th' old one away!
Here's Multiplication—
   So double the wine!
And here's to Division—
   That's yours, and this mine!

—WALLACE RICE

Observe, when Mother Earth is dry,
   She drinks the droppings of the sky,
And then the dewy cordial gives
   To every thirsty plant that lives.

The vapors which at evening sweep
   Are beverage to the swelling deep,

And when the rosy sun appears,
   He drinks the misty ocean's tears.

The moon, too, quaffs her paly stream
   Of lustre from the solar beam;
Then hence with all your sober thinking!
   Since Nature's holy law is drinking,
I'll make the law of Nature mine,
   And pledge the Universe in wine.

—TOM MOORE, *"The Universal Toast"*

O Water! Pure, free of pollution
I vainly wished that I dared trust it.
But I've an iron constitution,
And much I fear that water'd rust it.

—W. E. P. FRENCH

One sip of this will bathe the drooping spirits in delight
beyond the bliss of dreams.

—JOHN MILTON

One swallow doesn't make a summer, but it breaks a New
Year's resolution.

Take the glass away:—
   I know I hadn't oughter:—
I'll take a pledge—I will—
   I never will drink water.

—W. E. P. FRENCH

The corkscrew—a useful key to unlock the storehouse of wit, the treasury of laughter, the front door of fellowship, and the gate of pleasant folly.

—W. E. P. FRENCH

The first glass for myself; the second for my friends; the third for good humor, and the fourth for mine enemies.

—SIR WILLIAM TEMPLE, *first quoted in*
The Spectator *by Joseph Addison, October 13, 1711*

The man that isn't jolly after drinking
Is just a driveling idiot, to my thinking.

—EURIPIDES

Then fill the cup, fill high! fill high!
   Nor spare the rosy wine,
If death be in the cup, we'll die—
   Such death would be divine.

—JAMES RUSSELL LOWELL

There are several reasons for drinking,
And one has just entered my head;
If a man cannot drink when he's living
How the hell can he drink when he's dead?

There's naught, no doubt, so much the spirit calms as rum and true religion.

—LORD BYRON

'Tis a pity wine should be so deleterious,
For tea and coffee leave us much more serious.

—LORD BYRON

Too much is plenty.

—JOSEPH M. WEBER *and*
LEW FIELDS

To the cocktail party where olives are speared and friends
stabbed.

Within this goblet, rich and deep,
I cradle all my woes to sleep.

—TOM MOORE

SEE ALSO: *Beer/Ale; Biblical; Champagne; Mornings After; Revelry; Spirits;* ·
Wine

*There is an old tradition among those who collect limericks of using them
as toasts. All limericks work, and all that one has to do is change the
original first few words to "Here's to. . . ." For example:*

Here's to a lady from Guam
Who said, "Now the ocean's so calm
    I will swim, for a lark."
    She encountered a shark.
Let us now sing the ninetieth psalm.

Here's to a young woman named Bright,
Whose speed was much faster than light.
 She set out one day,
 In a relative way,
And returned on the previous night.

Here's to the young lady from Oak Knoll
Who thought it exceedingly droll
 At a masquerade ball
 Wearing nothing at all
To back in as a Parker House roll.

A Book of Verses underneath the Bough,
A Jug of Wine, a Loaf of Bread—and Thou
 Beside me singing in the Wilderness—
Oh, Wilderness were Paradise enow!

—EDWARD FITZGERALD,
from The Rubáiyát of Omar Khayyám

Because I love you truly,
Because you love me, too,
My very greatest happiness
Is sharing life with you.

Brew me a cup for a winter's night.
For the wind howls loud and the furies fight;
Spice it with love and stir it with care,
And I'll toast your bright eyes, my sweetheart fair.

—MINNA THOMAS ANTRIM

Come in the evening, or come in the morning,
Come when you are looked for, or come without warning,
A thousand welcomes you will find here before you,
And the oftener you come here the more I'll adore you.

—Irish

Come live with me, and be my love,
And we will all the pleasures prove,
That valleys, groves, or hills, or fields,
Or woods and steepy mountains yield.

—CHRISTOPHER MARLOWE, *"Passionate*
Shepherd to His Love"

Do you love me
Or do you not?
You told me once
But I forgot.

Give me a kisse, and to that kisse a score;
Then to that twenty, adde a hundred more;
A thousand to that hundred; so kiss on,
To make that thousand up a million;
Treble that million, and when that is done,
Let's kisse afresh, as when we first begun.

—ROBERT HERRICK, *"Hesperides"*

Here's to Dan Cupid, the little squirt,
He's lost his pants, he's lost his shirt,
He's lost most everything but his aim,
Which shows that love is a losing game.

Here's to fertility—the toast of agriculture and the bane of
love.

⁓ · · ⁓

132

Here's to love and unity,
Dark corners and opportunity.

Here's to Love, that begins with a fever and ends with a yawn.

Here's to love—with its billet-doux, bills and coos, biliousness,
bills, and bills of divorcement.

Here's to one and only one,
  And may that one be he
Who loves but one and only one,
  And may that one be me.

Here's to the land we love and the love we land.

Here's to the maid who is thrifty,
And knows it is folly to yearn,
And picks out a lover of fifty,
Because he has money to burn.

Here's to the pictures on my desk. May they never meet.

Here's to the prettiest, here's to the wittiest,
Here's to the truest of all who are true,
Here's to the neatest one, here's to the sweetest one,
Here's to them all in one—here's to you.

Here's to the wings of love—
  May they never moult a feather;
Till my big boots and your little shoes
  Are under the bed together.

Here's to the woman that I love
And here's to the woman that loves me,
And here's to all those that love her that I love,
And to those that love her that love me.

Here's to this water,
  Wishing it were wine,
Here's to you, my darling,
  Wishing you were mine.

Here's to those who love us,
  And here's to those who don't,
A smile for those who are willing to,
  And a tear for those who won't.

Here's to those who'd love us
  If we only cared;
Here's to those we'd love,
  If we only dared.

Here's to you,
May you live as long as you want to,
May you want to as long as you live.

Here's to you who halves my sorrows and doubles my joys.

I drink to your charm, your beauty and your brains—which
gives you a rough idea of how hard up I am for a drink.

—GROUCHO MARX

I have known many,
   liked a few,
Loved one—
   Here's to you!

I love you more than yesterday, less than tomorrow.

I would be friends with you and have your love.

If I were I, and you were you, would you?
There are times I would and times I wouldn't,
Times that I could and times I couldn't;
But the times I could and would and I felt game
Are the times I'm with you, dear.

If we cannot love unconditionally, love is already in a critical
condition.

—JOHANN WOLFGANG VON GOETHE

It warms me, it charms me,
To mention but her name,
It heats me, it beats me,
And sets me a' on flame.

—ROBERT BURNS

Let us be gay while we may
And seize love with laughter
I'll be true as long as you
But not for a moment after.

Let's drink to love,
Which is nothing—
Unless it's divided by two.

Love, and you shall be loved. All love is mathematically just,
as much as the two sides of an algebraic equation.

—RALPH WALDO EMERSON

Love doesn't make the world go 'round. Love is what makes
the ride worthwhile.

—FRANKLIN P. JONES

Love is what you've been through with somebody.

—JAMES THURBER

Love makes time pass—
Time makes love pass.

May love draw the curtain and friendship the cork.

May those now love
Who never loved before.
May those who've loved
Now love the more.

May we kiss those we please
And please those we kiss.

May we love as long as we live, and live as long as we love.

Mutual love, the crown of bliss.

—JOHN MILTON

Mystery and disappointment are not absolutely indispensable to the growth of love, but they are often very powerful auxiliaries.

—CHARLES DICKENS, Nicholas Nickleby

Say it with flowers
  Say it with eats,
Say it with kisses,
  Say it with sweets,
Say it with jewelry,
  Say it with drink,
But always be careful
  Not to say it with ink.

Thou hast no faults, or I no faults can spy;
Thou art all beauty, or all blindness I.

To each man's best and truest love—unless it be himself.

To every lovely lady bright,
I wish a gallant faithful knight;
To every faithful lover, too,
I wish a trusting lady true.

—SIR WALTER SCOTT

The love you give away is the only love you keep.

—ELBERT HUBBARD

They say there's microbes in a kiss,
This rumor is most rife,
Come lady dear, and make of me an invalid for life.

137

We'll drink to love, love, the one irresistible force that annihilates distance, caste, prejudice, and principles. Love, the pastime of the Occident, the passion of the East, Love, that stealeth upon us like a thief in the night, robbing us of rest, but bestowing in its place a gift more precious than the sweetest sleep. Love is the burden of my toast—here's looking at you.

Were't the last drop in the well,
    As I gasped upon the brink,
Ere my fainting spirit fell,
    'Tis to thee I would drink.

—LORD BYRON

Yesterday's yesterday while to-day's here,
To-day is to-day till to-morrow appear;
To-morrow's to-morrow until to-day's past—
And kisses are kisses as long as they last.

—OLIVER HERFORD

SEE ALSO: *Alliterative; Anniversary; Celia's Toast; General; Lust; Wedding*

A jolly good smoke, a nicely turned joke,
A handful of trumps when at play;
A drop of old wine, champagne that's fine,
And a run of good luck from today.

As you slide down the banister of life
May the splinters never face the wrong way.

138

Everything of fortune but her instability.

Good luck till we are tired of it.

I give you play days, hey days, and pay days!

May Dame Fortune ever smile on you;
    But never her daughter—
    Miss Fortune.

May the chicken never be hatched that will scratch on your
grave.

May we ever be able to part with our troubles to advantage.

May your luck be like the capital of Ireland, "Always Dublin."

May your luck ever spread, like jelly on bread.

No amount of planning can ever replace dumb luck!

Stately galleons there are,
    Laden deep with yellow gold;
Treasure argosies from far,
    Jewelled riches in their hold;
May they find a lucky star,
    Captains staunch, and sailors bold,
Not a storm or shoal to bar,

Not a blast of chill or cold
Till safe harbor they shall win—
Thus may all your ships come in!

—OLIVER MARBLE

Then welcome, stranger, cheer be thine,
If thou art a friend, of a friend of mine,
Here's luck. . . .

—JAMES MONROE MCLEAN,
The Book of Wine

To my friend—luck 'til the end!

SEE ALSO: *Better Times; Friendship; General; Irish*

Here's to Eve—mother of our race;
Who wore a fig leaf in just the right place.
And here's to Adam—daddy of us all;
Who was Johnny-on-the-spot,
When the leaves began to fall.

Here's to lying lips,
Though lying lips are bores,
But lying lips are mighty sweet
When they lie next to yours!

Here's to the game they call Ten Toes;
It's played all over town.
The girls all play with ten toes up,
The boys with ten toes down.

Here's to the girl who lives on the hill,
She won't but her sister will.
So here's to her sister.

Here's to the Hereafter.
If you're not here after
What I'm here after—
You'll be here a long time
After I'm gone.

Here's to the night I met you.
If I hadn't met you, I wouldn't have let you.
Now that I've let you, I'm glad that I met you.
And I'll let you again, I bet you!

Here's to you and here's to me,
And here's to the girl with the well-shaped knee.
Here's to the man with his hand on her garter;
He hasn't got far yet, but he's a damn good starter.

Here's to you, so sweet and good.
God made you; I wish I could.

Hogamus Higamus
Men are Polygamous
Higamous Hogamus
Women Monogamous.

It gives me great pleasure.

—GEORGE BERNARD SHAW, *when asked*
to give a toast on the subject of sex at a dinner party.

. . .

Sex: The pleasure is momentary; the expense is exorbitant;
the position ridiculous.

—G. K. CHESTERTON

The ocean is wide;
The sea is level.
Come to my arms
You little devil!

Today's the day,
Tonight's the night,
We've shot the stork—
So you're all right!

To your genitalia,
May they never jail-a-ya.

—*The University of Texas, 1950s*

SEE ALSO: *Love; Revelry; Special Occasions*

Here's to man—he is like a coal-oil lamp; he is not especially
bright; he is often turned down; he generally smokes; and he
frequently goes out at night.

Here's to that most provoking man
The man of wisdom deep
Who never talks when he takes his rest
But only smiles in his sleep.

Here's to the man that kisses his wife
And kisses his wife alone.
For there's many a man kisses another man's wife
When he ought to be kissing his own.
And here's to the man who kisses his child
And kisses his child alone.
For there's many a man kisses another man's child
When he thinks he is kissing his own.

Here's to you, Mister,
Whoever you may be.
For you're just the man of the evening,
And nothing more to me.

But, if you and your liquor should conquer,
And I fail to stand the test;
Well, here's to your technique, Mister,
I hope it's better than the rest.

I'll drink to the gentleman who I think
Is most entitled to it;
For if anyone ever can drive me to drink
He certainly can do it.

Man is somewhat like a sausage,
Very smooth upon the skin;
But you can never tell exactly
How much hog there is within.

Man is the only animal that laughs, drinks when he is not
thirsty, and makes love at all seasons of the year.

—VOLTAIRE

143

Men are like candles
They gleam and are bright
Men are like candles,
They shine best at night,
Men are like candles
They sputter about
And when they are needed
The darn things go out.

—CHARLIE JONES LAUGHBOOK, *May 1952*

Oh, here's to the good, and the bad men, too
For without them saints would have nothing to do!
Oh, I love them both, and I love them well,
But which I love better, I can never tell.

One must not become attached to animals: they do not last
long enough. Or to men: they last too long.

The Man We Love: He who thinks most good and speaks less
ill of his neighbor.

The men that women marry,
And why they marry them, will always be
A marvel and a mystery to the world.

—HENRY WADSWORTH LONGFELLOW

There is more felicity on the far side of baldness than young
men can possibly imagine.

—LOGAN PEARSALL SMITH

To the men I've loved
To the men I've kissed
My heartfelt apologies
To the men I've missed!

To Man: He is mad; he cannot make a worm, and yet he will be making gods by dozens.

—MONTAIGNE

Women's faults are many,
Men have only two—
Everything they say,
And everything they do.

SEE ALSO: *General; Husbands; Love; Lust; Parents; Weddings*

The most common American military toast is the army toast "How!" or, sometimes, "Here's how!" It has been in use for more than a hundred years. Several stories of its origin exist: 1) It came from the Sioux How kola, *which was an expression of friendship (and the basis for the caricature Indian who says "How"); 2) It dates to the Boxer Rebellion and the Chinese* Hao!; *3) It is a spoken symbol for water—H_2O—and whiskey—W—from which the "2" has been dropped.*

Traditionally, the navy has stressed a greater variety in its toasts as the following collecton shows.

A stout ship, a clear sea, and a far-off coast in stormy weather.

—*Navy*

Foes well tarred, and tars well feathered.

—*Navy*

Good ships, fair winds, and brave seamen.

—Navy

Grog, grub, and glory.

—Navy

Here's to bombers, may they get slower. And here's to fighter planes, may they grow swifter.

—CHARLES A. LINDBERGH, *Berlin, July
1936 (quoted in* Lindbergh, *by Leonard
Mosley, Doubleday, 1976)*

Here's to the ships of our navy
And the ladies of our land;
May the first be ever well rigged,
And the latter ever well manned.

—Navy

I give you muscles of steel, nerves of iron, tongues of silver, hearts of gold, necks of leather—the Marines.

Invincible in peace; invisible in war.

—"To the Militia"

Lots of beef and oceans of grog.

—Navy

May no son of the ocean be devoured by his mother.

—Navy

May rudders govern, and ships obey.

—Navy

Put out the red flag, and take ammunition on board.

—REAR ADM. ROBLEY D. EVANS

Put your trust in God, boys, and keep your powder dry.

—COLONEL BLACKER

Some wine, ho!
And let me the canakin clink, clink;
    And let me the canakin clink:
    A soldier's a man,
    A life's but a span;
Why then, let a soldier drink.

—SHAKESPEARE, Othello, *Act III*

The three generals in peace: General Peace, General Plenty, and General Satisfaction.

—*Army*

To a ten-inch gun: In life's great drama may you never play the part for which you have been cast!

To long lives and short wars!

—COLONEL POTTER, "*M*A*S*H*"
episode, February 4, 1980

147

The wind that blows, the ship that goes, and the lass that loves a sailor.

—*Navy*

True hearts and sound bottoms.

—*Navy*

SEE ALSO: *Historic*

mornings after

"**A** wet night maketh a dry morning,"
Quoth Hendyng, "rede ye right;
   And the cure most fair is the self-same hair
   Of the dog that gave the bit."

—"PUNDERSON"

Here's to the good time I must have had!

I wish that my room had a floor
I don't care so much for a door
But this walking around
Without touching the ground
Is getting to be quite a bore.

—GELETT BURGESS

If you'd known when you've enough
Of the punch and the claret cup
   It's time you quit the blessed stuff
When you fall down and can't get up.

Lord, how my head aches! What a head have I!
It beats as it would fall in twenty pieces.

—SHAKESPEARE, Romeo and Juliet

MACDUFF: What three things does drink especially provoke?
PORTER: Marry, sir, nose-painting, sleep, and urine.

—SHAKESPEARE, Macbeth

Not drunk is he who from the floor
Can rise again and drink some more;
But drunk is he who prostrate lies,
And who can neither drink nor rise.

—EUGENE FIELD

See the wine in the bowl, how it sparkles tonight.
Tell us what can compete with that red sea of light
Which breathes forth a perfume that deadens all sorrow,
And leaves us blessed now, with a headache tomorrow?

—DR. DORAN

149

Sing a song of sick gents,
Pockets full of rye,
Four and twenty highballs,
We wish that we might die.

The cocktail is a pleasant drink,
It's mild and harmless, I don't think!
 When you've had one, you call for two,
 And then you don't care what you do!
Last night I hoisted twenty-three
Of these arrangements into me;
My wealth increased, I swelled with pride;
I was pickled, primed, and ossified.
 R-e-m-o-r-s-e!
 Those dry martinis were too much for me.
 Last night at twelve I felt immense;
 To-day I feel like thirty cents.
At four I sought my whirling bed,
At eight I woke with such a head!
It is no time for mirth or laughter—
The cold, gray dawn of the morning after.

—GEORGE ADE, *from his poem,*
"R-E-M-O-R-S-E"

new year's

A song for the old, while its knell is tolled,
 And its parting moments fly!
But a song and a cheer for the glad New Year,
 While we watch the old year die!

—GEORGE COOPER

Another year is dawning! Let it be
For better or for worse, another year with thee.

As we start the New Year,
Let's get down on our knees
to thank God we're on our feet.

—Irish

Be at war with your voices, at peace with your neighbors, and let every new year find you a better man.

—BENJAMIN FRANKLIN

Here's to the bright New Year
    And a fond farewell to the old;
Here's to the things that are yet to come
    And to the memories that we hold.

Here's to you a New Year's Toast
May your Joy ne'er see a Sorrow's Ghost.

In the New Year,
may your right hand always be stretched out in friendship,
but never in want.

—Irish

In the year ahead,
May we treat our friends with kindness
and our enemies with generosity.

Let us resolve to do the best we can with what we've got.

—WILLIAM FEATHER

May all your troubles during the coming year be as short as
your New Year's resolutions.

May it be the best year yet for you
And everything prosper you may do.

May the best of this year be the worst of next.

May the Lord keep you in his hand
and never close his fist too tight on you.
And may the face of every good news
and the back of every bad news be toward us
in the New Year.

—Irish

May the new year help to make us old.

May the New Year bring summer in its wake.

—Irish

May the New Year grant you
the eye of a blacksmith on a nail
the good humor of a girl at a dance
the strong hand of a priest on his parish.

—Irish

May this sweetest oldtime greeting
   Heavily laden with good cheers
Bring content, and peace and plenty
   Enough to last through all the Year.

May your nets be always full—
your pockets never empty.
May your horse not cast a shoe
nor the devil look at you
in the coming year.

—Irish

New Year's Resolution:

Whatever you resolve to do,
  On any New Year's Day,
Resolve to yourself to be true
  And live—the same old way.

Ring out the old, ring in the new,
Ring happy bells across the snow;
The year is going, let him go.

—ALFRED LORD TENNYSON

Should auld acquaintance be forgot,
  And never brought to min',
Should auld acquaintance be forgot
  And days of auld lang syne.
For auld lang syne, my dear,
  For auld lang syne,
We'll tak' a cup o' kindness yet,
  For auld lang syne.

And here's a hand, my trusty fierce,
  And gie's a hand o' thine,
And we'll tak' a right guid willie-waught,
  For auld lang syne.
For auld lang syne, my dear,
  For auld lang syne,

We'll tak' a cup o' kindness yet,
    For auld lang syne.

And surely ye'll be your pint stowpt,
    And surely I'll be mine,
And we'll tak' a cup o' kindness yet,
    For auld lang syne.
For auld lang syne, my dear,
    For auld lang syne,
We'll tak' a cup o' kindness yet,
    For auld lang syne.

—ROBERT BURNS

Stir the eggnog, lift the toddy,
Happy New Year, everybody.

—PHYLLIS MCGINLEY

The New Year is ringing in,
May he be bringing in
The Good Times we've waited for so long in vain!
Without the demanding
All rise and drink standing,
And so say we all of us again and again.

The Old Man's dead. He was okay, maybe
But here's a health to the brand new baby.
I give you 19—.

To a firm hand for a flighty beast
an old dog for the long road
a kettle of fish for Friday
and a welcome for the New Year.

—Irish

Welcome be ye that are here,
Welcome all, and make good cheer,
Welcome all, another year.

Odd Customs

Many of the older toasting customs (such as drinking out of
the skull of a fallen enemy) are impractical in the context of
today's values, but here are three that you can still get away with.

1. There have always been drinking games and chal-
    lenges by which the loser must forfeit a glass—that
    is, have another drink. The following example
    comes from the very old English custom of drinking
    super negulum or "on the nail." The drinker must
    leave just the right amount of beer in his glass so that
    when it is poured out it just covers his fingernail. If
    too much or too little comes out, the penalty is to
    drink another glass.

Here's a health to Tom Brown,
Let the glass go round,
Drink up your ale without shrinking,
Put a pond on your nail,
And kiss the glass's tail,
And fill it up again without ceasing.

2. The Romans started the custom by which men drank
to the health of their women by having a drink for
each letter of their names. This has been translated
into modern terms:

Three cups to Amy, four to Kate be given,
To Susan five, six Rachel, Bridget seven.

Or, for the opposite sex:

It was not my plan to go on a bender,
But I just left Al for Alexander.

1. An old tavern amusement (with appropriate instruc-
tions):

This is my top. [Clink the top edges of the glasses.]
This is my bottom. [Clink the lower edges.]
And if you're nice to me,
I'll give you a little. [Pour some of your drink into the other
person's glass.]

SEE ALSO: *Glossary; Tongue Twisters; Ultimate Toasts*

old things

I drink as the fates ordain it.
  Come fill it and have done with rhymes.
Fill up the lovely glass and drain it
  In memory of dear old times.

—WILLIAM MAKEPEACE THACKERAY

I love everything that's old—old friends, old times, old manners, old books, old wine.

—OLIVER GOLDSMITH

Old wine is wholesomest, old pippins toothsomest,
Old wood burns brightest, old linen washes whitest,
Old soldiers' sweethearts are surest and old
Lovers are soundest.

—JOHN WEBSTER

Old wood to burn, old wine to drink,
old friends to trust,
and old authors to read.

—FRANCIS BACON

SEE ALSO: *Age*

parents

Father. May the love and respect we express toward him make up, at least in part, for the worry and care we have visited upon him.

He didn't tell me how to live;
he lived,
and let me watch him do it.

—CLARENCE BUDINGTON KELLAND

Here's to the happiest hours of my life—
Spent in the arms of another man's wife;
My mother!

To Life. The first half is ruined by our parents and the
second half by our children.

To Mother and Dad on their wedding anniversary:
We never know the love of our parents
for us till we have become parents.

—HENRY WARD BEECHER

To Mother—may she live long enough to forget what fiends
we used to be.

You may have a friend,
you may have a lover,
but don't forget,
your best friend is your mother.

—*Traditional autograph album inscription*

Farewell! a word that must be, and hath been—
A sound which makes us linger; yet—farewell.

—LORD BYRON

158

Friendly may we part and quickly meet again.

Happy are we met, happy have we been,
Happy may we part, and happy meet again.

Here's to good-byes—that they never be spoken!
Here's to friendships—may they never be broken!

It's hard for you-uns and we-uns;
It's hard for we-uns to part;
It's hard for you-uns and we-uns,
'Cause you-uns has we-uns's heart.

May we always part with regret and meet again with pleasure.

Must we part?
Well, if we must—we must—
And in that case
The less said the better.
                    —RICHARD B. SHERIDAN, The Critic, *Act II*

The pain of parting is nothing to the joy of meeting again.
                    —CHARLES DICKENS

'Tis grievous parting with good company.
                    —GEORGE ELIOT

True friendship's laws are by this rule express'd:
Welcome the coming, speed the parting guest.

                    —ALEXANDER POPE,
                    The Odyssey of Homer, *Book XIII*

SEE ALSO: *Friendship*

159

past, present, & future

Don't worry about the future,
  The present is all thou hast,
The future will soon be present,
  And the present will soon be past.

Every day should be passed
As though it were to be our last.

Here's to the present—and to hell with the past!
A health to the future and joy to the last!

May we always look forward with pleasure, and backward
with regret.

The cares of the day, old moralists say,
Are quite enough to perplex one;
Then drive today's sorrow away till tomorrow,
And then put it off till the next one.

—CHARLES DICKENS

The have-beens, the are-nows—and the may-bes!

This is the best day the world has ever seen.
Tomorrow will be better.

—R. A. CAMPBELL

Then fill the bowl—away with care,
  Our joy shall always last—

Our hopes shall brighten days to come,
    And memory gild the past.

—TOM MOORE

SEE ALSO: *Age; Anniversaries; Parting; Weddings*

professional & occupational

Agriculture

Aye, the corn, the Royal Corn,
Within whose yellow heart
There is health and strength for all the nations.

—GOVERNOR R. J. OGLESBY of Illinois

Blessed be Agriculture! If one does not have too much
of it.

—CHARLES DUDLEY WARNER

Fat cattle, green fields, and many a bushel in your barn.

—Irish

God speed the plough,
But keep me from the handles!

—Yorkshire toast

Good luck to the hoof and the horn
Good luck to the flock and the fleece
Good luck to the growers of corn
With blessings of plenty and peace.

May we spring up like vegetables, have turnip-noses, radish cheeks, and carroty hair, and may our hearts never be hard, like those of cabbages, nor may we be rotten at the core.

Some people tell us there ain't no hell,
But they never farmed, so how can they tell?*

Success to the farmers of America—may they always reap a golden harvest.

To Farmers—founders of civilization.

—DANIEL WEBSTER

Baking

May we never be done so much as to make us crusty.

Barbering

He cuts our hair
And shaves our face,
And talks and talks
With ease and grace.

Business

A man should be honest and upright and true—
  No divvy nor graft nor dishonest intent;
But unless he's a chump who cannot catch on
  He'll find out a way to make thirty percent.

—M. QUAD

* This has been adapted to other fields, such as mining.

Good trade and well paid.

May the weight of our taxes never bend the back of our credit.

Our mints: The only places that make money without advertising.

Though confidence is very fine,
   And makes the future sunny;
I want no confidence in mine,
   I'd rather have the money.

Cooking

May we always have more occasion for the cook than for the doctor.

God sends meat, the devil sends cooks.

—CHARLES VI

Dentistry

'Twould make a suffering mortal grin,
   And laugh away dull care,
If he could see his dentist in
   Another dentist's chair.

To the Dentist:
Who, East, West, North and South,
Always lives from hand to mouth.

Firefighting

Good attachment, free plugs, full pumps, and fair play to all true firemen.

May he never be *toasted* save by the glass of his friends.

Our Fire Department—the army that draws water instead of blood, and thanks instead of tears.

Gardening

Great God of little things
Look upon my labours
Make my little garden
A little better than my neighbor's!

General

An honest lawyer, a pious divine, and a skillful physician.

May the work that you have
Be the play that you love!

—E. GERBERDING

Oh let us love our occupations,
Bless the squire and his relations,
Live upon our daily rations,
And always know our proper stations.

—CHARLES DICKENS

The Law

A bad compromise beats a good lawsuit.

And do as adversaries do in law—
Strive mightily, but eat and drink as friends.

        —SHAKESPEARE, The Taming of the Shrew, *Act I*

A bumper of good liquor
Will end a contest quicker
Than justice, judge, or vicar;
So fill a cheerful glass,
And let good humor pass.

        —RICHARD B. SHERIDAN, The Duenna, *Act II*

A countryman between two lawyers is like a fish between two cats.

        —BENJAMIN FRANKLIN

Fond of doctors, little health;
Fond of lawyers, little wealth.

Here's a toast to a man of great trials and many convictions.

Justice while she winks at crimes,
Stumbles on innocence sometimes.

        —SAMUEL BUTLER

Litigious terms, fat contentions, and flowing fees.

        —JOHN MILTON

May the depths of our potations never cause us to let judgment go by default.

May the judgments of our Benches never be biased.

May we always lie upon our left sides, since the law will not permit us to sleep on our rights.

The glorious uncertainty of the law.

—First found in Macklin's Loveala Mode *(1759).*
Ever since, it has been used as a toast at legal dinners.

The law: It has honored us; may we honor it.

—DANIEL WEBSTER

The lawyer—a learned gentleman, who rescues your estate from your enemies, and keeps it himself.

To Lawyers: You cannot live without the lawyers, and certainly you cannot die without them.

—JOSEPH H. CHOATE

"Virtue in the middle," said the Devil, as he seated himself between two lawyers.*

When a festive occasion our spirit unbends
We should never forget the profession's best friends.
So we'll pass round the wine
And a light bumper fill
To the jolly testator who makes his own will.

Who taught me first to litigate,
My neighbor and my brother hate,
And my own rights overrate?
  My lawyer.

---

* This toast sometimes ends with the word "editors."

Who lied to me about his case,
And said we'd have an easy race,
And did it all with solemn face?
    My client.

Medicine

And Nathan, being sick, trusted not in the lord, but sent for a physician—and Nathan was gathered unto his fathers.

—OLD TESTAMENT

The doctors are our friends, let's please them well,
For though they kill but slow they are certain.

—FRANCIS BEAUMONT *and*
JOHN FLETCHER

To mankind we drink:—'tis a pleasant task:
Heaven bless it and multiply its wealth;
But it is a little too much to ask
That we should drink to its health.

Unto our doctors let us drink,
    Who cure our chills and ills,
No matter what we really think
    About their pills and bills.

—PHILIP MCALLISTER

When Judgment Day arrives and all
The doctors answer for their sins,
O' think of what they'll get who bring
The howling triplets and the twins.

Mining

May all your labors be in vein.

—*Yorkshire miner's toast*

Novice

Here's to learning the ropes without coming unraveled.

Police

Here's to the policeman who passes our way.
Here's to the mailman who calls every day.
Here's to the babies who continually say:
"Mom, which is my daddy—the blue or the gray?"

Politics

Here's to the honest politician—a man who when bought
stays bought.

The Press

A health to the slaves of the ink-pot,
   Who, careless of fortune or fame,
Will give their best years (missing brilliant careers)
   And all for the love of the game!

—JAMES P. HAVERSON

Here's to the Press—The "tongue" of the country; may it
never be cut out.

The liberty of the press and success to its defenders.

The Newspaper—may it fight like an army in the defense of right with strong columns and good leaders.

The Press of Our Country: The engine of our liberty, the terror of tyrants, and the schoolmaster of the whole world.

The Press: the great bulwark of our liberties, and may it ever remain unshackled.

—American, eighteenth century

The Press: the great corrector of abuses, the shield of the oppressed, and the terror of the oppressor.

We editors may dig and toil
   Till our fingertips are sore,
But some poor fish is sure to say,
"I've heard that joke before."

Printing

The master of all trades: he beats the farmer with his fast "hoe," the carpenter with his "rule," and the mason in "setting up his columns"; he surpasses the lawyer and the doctor in attending to the "cases," and beats the person in the management of the devil.

You can always tell a barber
  By the way he parts his hair;
You can always tell a dentist
  When you're in the dentist's chair;
And even a musician—
  You can tell him by his touch;
You can always tell a printer,
  But you cannot tell him much.

A Promotion

Here's to becoming top banana without losing touch with the bunch.
                                    —BILL COPELAND *in the* Sarasota Journal

Psychiatry

Here's to my psychiatrist.
He finds you cracked and leaves you broke.

Sales

Here's to us. Never sell a salesman short.

Let's drink to my sales manager's health so I'll have a reason
to put these on my expense account.
                                    —*Cartoon caption,* Esquire, *April 1955*

Securities

He keeps us poor all our lives so we can die rich.

Waitering

We drink your health, O Waiter!
  And may you be preserved
From old age, gout, or sudden death!—
  At least till supper's served.

—OLIVER HERFORD and
JOHN CECIL CLAY, "Happy Days"

Writing

Authors are judged by strange, capricious rules,
The great ones are thought mad, the small ones fools.

The writer's very good health. May he live to be as old as his jokes!

To an American author: Though a true democrat, may you always keep within touch of royalty!

Writing is a dog's life, but the only life worth living.

—GUSTAVE FLAUBERT

SEE ALSO: *Special People*

Quotes (which are not exactly toasts but which belong in a book like this)

. . .

Do not worry; eat three square meals a day; say your prayers; be courteous to your creditors; keep your digestion good; exercise; go slow, and easy. Maybe there are other things that your special case requires to make you happy, but, my friend, these I reckon will give you a good lift.

—ABRAHAM LINCOLN

House Rules. The bar of the National Press Club in Washington, D.C., once displayed a quotation from the Holy Rule of St. Benedict, a directive for conduct issued by the early monastic order:

> If any pilgrim monk come from distant parts, with wish as a guest to dwell in the monastery, and will be content with the customs which he finds in the place, and do not perchance by his lavishness disturb the monastery, but is simply content with what he finds, he shall be received for as long a time as he desires. If, indeed, he find fault with anything, or expose it, reasonably, and with the humility of charity, the Abbot shall discuss it prudently, lest perchance God had sent him for this very thing. But, if he have been found gossipy and contumacious in the time of his sojourn as guest, it shall be said to him, honestly, that he must depart. If he does not go, let two stout monks, in the name of God, explain the matter to him.

. . . .

I feel no pain dear mother now,
But Oh I am so dry.
O take me to a brewery
And leave me there to die.

—ANONYMOUS

I kissed my first woman and smoked my first cigarette on the same day. I have never had time for tobacco since.

—ARTURO TOSCANINI

I really don't deserve this. But I have arthritis and don't deserve that either.

—JACK BENNY *on accepting an award*

In the sixteenth century when there were no Water Boards, water was really dangerous to drink; everybody in England drank ale, beer and wine. England's population then was less than the population of London to-day, and the quota of great statesmen, soldiers, sailors, philosophers, poets and dramatists reared on beer and wine in those days compares favourably with the greatness reached in our own sober times.

—A. L. SIMMONS, Daily Telegraph,
April 1931

Leave the flurry
To the masses;
Take your time
And shine your glasses.

—*Old Shaker verse*

Mankind are earthen jugs with spirits in them.

—NATHANIEL HAWTHORNE

Saw a wedding in the church and strange to see what delight we married people have to see these poor fools decoyed into our condition.

—*Entry in Samuel Pepys's* Diary *for December 25, 1665*

The best audience is one that is intelligent, well educated—and a little drunk.

—VICE PRESIDENT ALBEN W. BARKLEY

This North American has been an inmate of my 'ouse ove two weeks, yit he hasn't made no attempts to scalp any member of my family. He hasn't broke no cups or sassers, or furniture of any kind. (Hear, hear.) I find I can trust him with lighted candles. He eats his vittles with a knife and fork. people of this kind should be encurridged. I purpose is 'elth. (Loud 'plaws.)

—*To* ARTEMUS WARD, *from* Punch, *1866*

This wine is too good for toast-drinking, my dear. You don't want to mix emotions up with a wine like that. You lose the taste.

—COUNT MIPPIPOPLOUS *to Brett in* The Sun Also Rises *by Ernest Hemingway*

There must be more beer, cheaper beer, better beer! People who do not drink beer do not realize that beer is as important to the working classes as bread. . . . Men who find they cannot get beer tend to develop a taste for less innocent liquors. Good ale and good beer are drinks of temperate men, and it must be confessed that England has bred a race of mighty fighting men on her national brew. Good beer is the basis of true temperance.

—Daily Express, *January 25, 1919*

To Minerva
From the Greek

My temples throb, my pulses boil,
  I'm sick of Song and Ode and Ballad—
So Thyrsis, take the midnight oil,
  And pour it on a lobster salad.

When Woodrow proposed to me I was so surprised I nearly
fell out of bed.

—Attributed to the second Mrs. Woodrow Wilson

Who buys good land buys many stones,
Who buys good meat buys many bones,
Who buys good eggs buys many shells,
Who buys good ale buys nothing else.

—GRAMMER GURTON'S NEEDLE

SEE ALSO: *Secrets*

Here's a health in homely rhyme
To our oldest classmate, Father Time;
May our last survivor live to be
As bold and wise and as thorough as he!

—OLIVER WENDELL HOLMES

Here's to all of us!
For there's so much good in the worst of us
  And so much bad in the best of us,
That it hardly behooves any of us,
  To talk about the rest of us.

Some among many gather again,
A glass to their happiness; friendship,
Amen. . . .
The Survivors.

—JAMES MONROE MCLEAN, The Book of Wine

Then fill the cup, fill high! fill high!
  Let joy our goblets crown,
We'll bung Misfortune's scowling eye,
  And knock Foreboding down.

—JAMES RUSSELL LOWELL, *from*
"To the Class of '38"

To friends: As long as we are able
To lift our glasses from the table.

To the good old days . . . we weren't
so good, 'cause we weren't so old!

SEE ALSO: *Colleges and Universities; Friendship; Parting; Past, Present, and Future*

A very merry, dancing, drinking,
Laughing, quaffing, and unthinking time.

—JOHN DRYDEN

Alcohol—a liquid good for preserving almost anything except secrets.

—GIDEON WORDZ

And the night shall be filled with music,
And the cares that infest the day
Shall fold their tents like the Arabs,
And as silently steal away.

—HENRY WADSWORTH LONGFELLOW

But, fill me with the old familiar juice,
Methinks I might recover bye and bye.

—OMAR KHAYYÁM

Care to our coffin adds a nail, no doubt,
And every grain, so merry, draws one out.

—JOHN WOLCOTT

Drink to the girls and drink to their mothers,
Drink to their fathers and to their brothers;
Toast their dear healths as long as you're able,
And dream of their charms while under the table.

Drinking will make a man quaff,
Quaffing will make a man sing,
Singing will make a man laugh,
And laughing long life doth bring.

—THOMAS D'URFEY

Fill up the bowl, upon my soul,
Your trouble you'll forget, sir;
If it takes more, fill twenty more,
Till you have drowned regret, sir.

Fill up the goblet and reach me some,
Drinking makes wise, but dry feasting makes glum.

—Oriental

Here is a riddle most abstruse:
  Cans't read the answer right?
Why is it that my tongue grows loose
  Only when I grow tight?

Here, waiter, more wine, let me sit while I'm able,
Till all my companions sink under the table.

—OLIVER GOLDSMITH

Here's pleasure as you like it.

Here's to a guy who is never blue,
Here's to a buddy who is ever true,
Here's to a pal, no matter what the load,
Who never declines one for the road.

Here's to a long life and a merry one,
A quick death and an easy one,
A pretty girl and a true one,
A cold bottle and another one.

I'm tired of drinking toasts
For each small glass of gin.
Let's toss out all the hooey
And toss the liquor in.

In for a high old frolic,
Chiefly alcoholic.

Laugh at all things,
Great and small things,
Sick and well, at sea or shore;
While we are quaffing,
Let's have laughing.
Who the devil cares for more?

—LORD BYRON

Let us have wine and women, mirth and laughter
Sermons and soda water the day after.

—LORD BYRON

Let us sip and let it slip
   And go which way it will-a
Let us trip and let us ship
   And let us drink our fill-a.

Let's live in haste; use pleasures while we may:
Could life return, 'twould never lose a day.

—ROBERT HERRICK

The more I drink, the better I sing.

Said Aristotle unto Plato,
   "Have another sweet potato?"
Said Plato unto Aristotle,
   "Thank you, I prefer the bottle."

—OWEN WISTER

Raise your glasses, lift them high,
Drink to health dear toasters;
But when you set them down again,
Can't you hit our coasters?

—D. S. HALACY, JR., 1000 Jokes,
May-July 1955, "The Ringleavers"

There are many good reasons for drinking,
One has just entered my head
If a man doesn't drink when he's living,
How the hell can he drink when he's dead?

They tell me my love would in time have been cloy'd,
And that Beauty's insipid when once 'tis enjoyed;
But in wine I both time and enjoyment defy,
For the longer I drink the more thirsty am I.

Too much work, and no vacation,
Deserves at least a small libation.
So hail! my friends, and raise your glasses;
Work's the curse of the drinking classes.

Toss the pot, toss the pot; let us be merry,
And drink till our cheeks be red as a cherry.

—ANONYMOUS, *circa 1600*

Turn out more ale, turn up the light;
I will not go to bed tonight.
Of all the foes that man should dread
The first I have had both old and young,
And ale we drank and songs we sung;

Enough you know when this is said,
That, one and all—they died in bed!

—CHARLES HENRY WEBB,
Dum Vivimus Vigilamus

What would you like to drink to?
To about three in the morning.

Who loves not women, wine, and song,
Remains a fool his whole life long.

—JOHANN HEINRICH VOSS

You're a purty man!—you air!
With a pair o' eyes like two fried eggs
An' a nose like a Bartlutt Pear!

SEE ALSO: *Beer/Ale; Champagne; Libations; Lust; Mornings After; Spirits;
Ultimate Toasts; Wine*

May the Irish hills caress you.
May her lakes and rivers bless you.
May the luck of the Irish enfold you.
May the blessings of St. Patrick behold you.

May the Leprechauns be near you to spread luck along your
    way
And may all the Irish angels smile upon you on St. Pat's Day.

On St. Patrick's Day you should spend time with saints and scholars, so you know I have two more stops to make.

—*St. Patrick's Day toast delivered to Speaker*
Jim Wright on Capitol Hill, 1988

Saint Patrick was a gentleman,
　Who, through strategy and stealth,
Drove all the snakes from Ireland—
　Here's a bumper to his health.
But not too many bumpers,
　Lest we lose ourselves, and then
Forget the good Saint Patrick,
　And see the snakes again.

Success attend St. Patrick's fist,
　For he's a saint so clever;
Oh! he give the snakes and toads a twist,
　He banished them forever.

The anniversary of St. Patrick's day—and may the Shamrock be green forever.

SEE ALSO: *Irish*

A guid New Year to yin and a'
　And mony may you see,
And may the mouse ne'er run out o'
　Your girnel wi' a tear in its 'e.

Blythe may we a' be,
Ill may we never see!

Here's grand luck, an' muckle fat weans [big, fat children]!

Here's health ta the seeck, an' stilts ta the lame;
Claise ta the back, an' brose ta the wame [gruel to the belly]!

Here's tae auld Scotland, the land o' our birth,
Wi' its hulls where stormy winds whistle.
Ye can sit for a month on the shamrock an' the rose,
But ye canna sit land on the thistle!

Here's tae us! Wha's like us?
    Da' few and they're deed.
[Here's to us! Who's like us?
    Damn few and they're dead.]

Here's to them that lo'es us, or lends us a lift.

May the best ye've ever seen
Be the worst ye'll ever see.

May the mouse ne'er leave our meal pock wi' the tear
in its ee.

May the winds o' adversity ne'er blaw open our door.

May your life
Be like good Scotch
Smooth and clear
    And like good Scotch
May it improve
With every passing year.

O, wad, some pow'r the giftie gie us
To see oursels as others see us!
It wad frae money a blunder free us.

—ROBERT BURNS

The deil rock them in the creel that does na' wish us a' weel.

Then let us toast John Barleycorn,
  Each man a glass in hand;
And may his great posterity
  Ne'er fail in old Scotland!

Up wi' yer glesses, an' deil tak the hindmaist!

SEE ALSO: *New Years; Ultimate Toasts*

Secrets

A collection of ancestral information which has been lost to the modern world.

Eight Conditions of Overindulgence
(From *Pierce Penniless* by Thomas Nashe, 1592)

The first is Ape drunke, and he leapes, and sings, and, daunceth for the heauens: the second is Lion drunke, and he flings the pots about the house, calls his Hostesse whore, breakes the glasse windowes with his dagger, and is apt to quarrell with any man that speaks to him. The third is Swine drunke, heavy, lumpish and sleepy. The fourth is Sheepe drunk, wise in his own conceit, when he cannot bring forth a right word. The fifth is Mawdlin drunk, when a fellow weep for kindness in the middle of his ale, and kiss you saying "By God Captain I love you." The sixth is Martin drunke, when a man is drunke and drinks himself sober ere he stir. The seventh is Goat drunk—with his mind on naught but lechery. The eight is Foxe drunke, when he is craftie drunk, as many of the Dutch men be, will never bargain but when they ave drunk.

Six Ways to Prevent Intoxication
(From *Valuable Secrets Concerning Arts and Trades*, 1795)

1. Take white cabbage's, and four pomegranate's juices, two ounces of each, with one of vinegar. Boil all together for some time to the consistence of a syrup. Take one ounce of this before you are going to drink, and drink afterwards as much, and as long, as you please.
2. Eat five or six bitter almonds fasting; this will have the same effect.
3. It is affirmed that if you eat mutton or goat's lungs roasted; cabbage, or any feed; or wormwood, it will absolutely prevent the bad effects which result from the excess of drinking.
4. You may undoubtedly prevent the accidents resulting from hard drinking, if before dinner you eat, in salad, four or five tops of raw cabbages.
5. Take some swallows' beaks, and burn them in a crucible. When perfectly calcined crush them on a stone, and put some of that powder in a glass of wine, and drink it. Whatever wine you may drink to excess afterwards, it will have no effect upon you. The whole body of the swallow, prepared in the same manner, will have the same effect.
6. Pound in a mortar the leaves of a peach-tree, and squeeze the juice of them in a basin. Then, fasting, drink a full glass of that liquor, and take whatever excess of wine you will on that day, you will not be intoxicated.

Three Mongol Secrets for Tippling
(From *The Imperial Cookery Book of the Mongol Dynasty*)

1. Never force yourself to eat, and never get angry, when you are under the influence of drink or you will break out in boils. Washing the face in cold water has the same effect.
2. Don't ride or jump about, or exert yourself in any way when drunk or you will injure your bones and sinews and undermine your strength.
3. If you see in your wine the reflection of a person not in your range of vision, don't drink it.

How to Reform Those Who Drink Too Much Wine
(From *Valuable Secrets Concerning Arts and Trades*, 1795)

Put in a sufficient quantity of wine three or four large eels, which leave there till quite dead. Give that wine to drink to the person you want to reform, and he or she will be so much disgusted of wine, that tho' they formerly made much use of it, they will now have quite an aversion to it.

To Refresh a Large Number of People
(From *Inns, Ales, and Drinking Customs of Old England*, by Frederick W. Hackwood, 1909)

In 1694 Admiral Edward Russell, commanding the Mediterranean fleet, gave a grand entertainment at Alicant. The tables were laid under the shade of orange trees in four garden walks meeting at a common centre, where there stood a handsome marble fountain. This fountain was converted for the occasion into a gigantic punch-bowl. Four hogsheads of brandy, one pipe of Malaga wine, twenty gallons of lime-juice, twenty-five hundred lemons, thirteen hundred-weight of fine white sugar, five pounds' weight of grated nutmegs, three hundred toasted biscuits, and eight hogsheads of water, formed the ingredients of this monster potation. An elegant canopy placed over the potent liquor prevented waste by evaporation or dilution by rain. To crown this titanic effort, a small boy was placed in a boat expressly built for the purpose, to row round the fountain and assist in landing the punch into the cups of the six thousand persons who were invited to partake of it.

To Properly Toast Another
(From *The Irish Hubbub, or the English Hue and Crie,* Barnabe Rich, 1617)

He that beginnes the health hath prescribed orders; first uncovering his head he takes a full cup in his hand, and settling his countenance with a grave aspect, he crave an audience; silence being once obtained, he begins to breathe out the name peradventure of some honourable personage, that was worthy of a better regard than to have his name polluted at so unfitting a time, amongst a company of drunkards, but his health is drunk to, and he that pledges must likewise off with his cap, kisse his fingers, and bow himself in sign of reverent acceptance. When the leader sees his follower thus prepared, he sups up his breath, turns the bottom of his cup upward, and in ostentation of his dexteritie gives the cup a phillip to make it cry *twange,* and thus the first scene is acted.

Drink Formula Calling for One (1) Cow Ale Syllabub

(Eighteenth-century England)

Place in a large bowl a quart of strong ale or beer, grate into it a little nutmeg, and sweeten it with sugar. Milk the cow rapidly into the bowl, forcing the milk as strongly as possible into the ale, and against the sides of the vessel, to raise a good froth. Let it stand for an hour and will then be fit for use. Cider may be used instead of ale, and the sugar should be proportioned to the taste of the drinker.

Recipe for an After-dinner Speech

Three long breaths.
Compliment to the audience.
Funny story.
Outline of what speaker is *not* going to say.
Points that he will touch on later.
Two Bartlett's Familiar Quotations.
Outline of what speaker *is* going to say.
Points that he has not time to touch on now.
Reference to what he said first.
Funny story.
Compliment to the audience.
Ditto to our City, State, and Country.
Applause.
N.B. For an oration, use same formula, repeating each
sentence three times in slightly different words.

—MARY ELEANOR ROBERTS

A Selected Toast and
Tipple Glossary

Some special terms for special occasions.

absinthe Makes the heart grow fonder.

all nations A vile drink composed of the dregs of various casks to which strong beer was sometimes added.

beverage Derives from the word *bever,* which is a drink taken between meals. There used to be bever days at Eton College, for instance, when extra beer was served to the students.

binder The last drink of the evening.

bridal We all know what this means, but what is interesting is that it comes from an old English custom of the "Bride-Ale" by which the bride was given the proceeds from the sale of ale at her wedding.

brimmer A glass so full that the liquid touches the brim. Although the liquid has climbed to the brim, there is a slight depression or hollow in the center of the surface. A *bumper* (see below) is a brimmer to which extra drops have been added to fill the hollow to a bump. The difference between a brimmer and a bumper can be demonstrated by floating a cork fragment on the surface. In a brimmer the cork will float to the edge, while it will sit in the middle of a bumper.

bumper A glass filled to the extreme. Bumpers are often used in toasting and sometimes taken in one draught. There are two explanations for the term: 1) It comes from the French *au bon pe,* or "good father," and is attributed to the medieval custom of dedicating the first cup of wine to the Pope. 2) It comes from a glass filled so high that the liquid "bumps" up in the middle, higher in the center than at the brim. (See *brimmer,* above.)

drop There are 60 drops in a teaspoon; 120 in a dessertspoon; 240 in a tablespoon; 480 in an ounce; 960 in a wineglass; 1,920 in a teacup; 3,840 in a breakfast-cup or tumbler; 7,680 in a pint; 15,360 in a quart; 61,440 in a gallon; 2,935,360 in a barrel; 3,870,720 in a hogshead. Its equivalent weight is .9493 grams. A drop is equal to a minim. (From *The Banquet Book* by Cuyler Reynolds, 1902)

flap-dragon An Elizabethan drink with a flammable surface, ignited for hard drinkers to quaff in one fast gulp. Drinking these was called flap-dragoning, and there are several references to the custom in Shakespeare's works.

fob   Brewer's term for beer froth.

hobnob   The quaint custom of sitting around the "hob," or projecting corner of a fireplace, and drinking.

loving cup   A massive common cup, passed from hand to hand as a token of peace. It usually has three handles. Today these are largely ornamental and used as trophies. There are a number of stories purporting to state the origin of the loving cup. This one makes as much sense as the rest and is the most interesting explanation: It seems that King Henry V was out riding, became thirsty, and stopped at the door of a country inn for a cup of wine. The barmaid handed it to him by its single handle, forcing him to take it in both hands, thereby soiling his gloves. The king made up his mind that this would not happen again so he had a cup made with two handles, which he then had sent to the inn for his private use. When he next happened on the inn, he again ordered a cup of wine. The same barmaid served him, this time grasping the cup by its two handles. The problem was solved when he ordered a three-handled cup made.

Nebuchadnezzar   Until 1986 the largest size of champagne bottle, capable of holding 104 glasses. It is larger than the 83-glass *Balthazar*, 62-glass *Salmanazar*, 41-glass *Methusela*, 31-glass *Rehoboam*, 21-glass *Jeroboam* and 10-glass *Magnum*. Your standard *Bottle* holds a mere 5 glasses. See *Salomon*, below.

nip   One-sixth of a quartern (a five-ounce measure).

noggin   An old ale measure for a quarter-pint. The word appears in old drinking songs such as one with this currently relevant line:

> Before we think of jogging,
>
> Let's take a cheerful noggin.

no heel taps   An old drinking injunction meaning to finish your glass—leave no dregs.

piggin   A drinking vessel made from a pig's skin. It is one of a number of leather vessels of yore including also the bombard, gaspin, and black jack. Other bygone vessels include the crinze (earthenware), the wooden mazer, and the quaich (silver or china). In former times, it seems that just about anything that you could find might end up as a cup. A writer of 1635 tells of all the predictable materials for drinking vessels, including old boots, and then adds, "We have, besides, cups made out of

hornes of beasts, of cockernuts, of goords, of the eggs of os-
triches; others made of the shells of diverse fishes, brought from
the Indies and other places, and shining like mother-of-pearle."

pitcher Pouring vessel originally made of leather and so called
because it was lined with pitch to make it waterproof.

pony A glass holding about a mouthful of spirits.

punch Although used less specifically today, the word originally referred to a drink of five ingredients: liquor, water, lemon,
sugar, and spice. It derives from the Hindu word.

puncheon A wine measure equal to 2 tierces, or 84 gallons, or
336 quarts, or 672 pints.

roast Different than a toast, viz.,

> When T stands for tender
>
> And R stands for rough
>
> You've the difference twixt a
>
> Toast and a Roast.

—STANLICUS

Salomon As of 1986 the largest champagne bottle ever pro-
duced. Capable of containing the equivalent of 24 normal 750-
milliliter bottles, seven of them were mouth-blown in France on
the occasion of the Centennial of
the Statue of Liberty.

stirrup cup One for the
road. The name given to
the drink given to a
departing guest whose feet
were already in the stirrups.

teetotaler Term comes from a
pledge of a Michigan temperance society of the 1830s.
Members were offered
two pledges: one
calling for moderate
drinking, the other
calling for total
abstinence. Once on
the membership rolls, the
moderates were identified as
"O.P." for "Old Pledge," and

191

"T-Total" if they swore off entirely. They were soon known as teetotalers.

toast The only thing that can be eaten or drunk.

toddy A sweet drink of whiskey, water, and sugar that is often warmed. Toddy is a corruption of *taudi*, the Hindu name for a sweet palm juice.

tumbler A common drinking glass that was originally a drinking horn unevenly weighted with lead at the bottom. This was done to encourage the drinker to drain the contents at one draught, as the vessel was so weighted that it could not be put down without tumbling over. The tumbler is believed to be of Saxon origin.

water Liquid of which ice is made.

wet your whistle To drink. The term reputedly came from an old Scottish custom of awarding a silver whistle to the winner of a drinking contest. These contests were decided when only one participant was left standing and able to blow the whistle. One such contest was won by a Scotch nobleman who bested a boastful Dane after several days and nights of drinking. Robert Burns wrote of the memorable contest:

> I sing of a Whistle, a Whistle of worth;
>
> I sing of a Whistle, the pride of the North
>
> Was brought to the Court of our good Scottish King,
>
> And long with this Whistle all Scotland shall ring.

SEE ALSO: *Ultimate Toasts*

Here's health to my soul and health to my heart,

Where this is going, there's gone many a quart.

Through my teeth and round my gums;

Look out, belly, here it comes!

Here's to ourselves
And wishing all
The wish they wish themselves!

Here's to the health of those we love best—
Our noble selves—God bless us;
None better and many a damn sight worse.
Drink to-day, and drown all sorrow;
You shall, perhaps, not do it to-morrow.

—FRANCIS BEAUMONT *and* JOHN FLETCHER

Here's to you,
  And here's to me;
But as you're not here,
  Here's two to me.

Life is a banquet and most poor sons-of-bitches are starving
to death.

—PATRICK DENNIS, Auntie Mame

Our noble selves—may we never be less.

Our noble selves—why not toast ourselves, and praise
ourselves; since we have the best means of knowing all the
good in ourselves.

Well! Here's luck, great luck,
Such luck as never was known;
May the winner's pockets bulge with coin,
And these pockets be—my own.

shakespearean

A flock of blessings light upon thy back.

—Romeo and Juliet, *Act III*

A health, gentlemen,
Let it go round.

—Henry VIII, *Act I*

Come, come, good wine is a good familiar creature, if it be
well used; exclaim no more against it.

—Othello, *Act II*

Drink down all unkindness.

—The Merry Wives of Windsor, *Act I*

Fair thought and happy hours attend on you.

—The Merchant of Venice, *Act III*

Fill the cup and let it come,
I'll pledge you a mile to the bottom.

—Henry IV, Part II, *Act III*

Frame your mind to mirth and merriment,
Which bars a thousand harms and lengthens life.

—The Taming of the Shrew, *Act II*

God's benison go with you; and with those
That would make good of bad, and
friends of foes.

—Macbeth, *Act II*

I wish all good befortune you!
—The Two Gentlemen of Verona, *Act IV*

I wish you all the joy you can wish.
—The Merchant of Venice, *Act III*

Let's drink together friendly, and embrace.
—Henry IV, Part II, *Act IV*

Love sought is good, but given unsought
is better.
—Twelfth Night, *Act III*

Speak no more of her. Give me a bowl
of wine:
In this I bury all unkindness, Cassius.
—BRUTUS *to Cassius, in the tent scene
of* Julius Caesar

The best of happiness, honor, and fortunes keep with you.
—Timon of Athens, *Act I*

They do not love that do not show their love.
—The Two Gentlemen of Verona, *Act I*

To make the coming hour o'erflow and joy,
And pleasure drown the brim.
—All's Well That Ends Well, *Act II*

You have deserved his commendation, true applause and
love.
—As You Like It, *Act I*

Skoaling

Scandinavian toasting hinges for the most part on one word, skål, *or as it has been anglicized,* skoal. *It is a particular kind of toasting with its own protocol. For starters, one is supposed to engage the eyes of the person toasted and keep the gaze locked until the act is completed and the glass returned to a point below the neck. One must also know when to skoal. The Swedish Information Service provides these guidelines for anyone planning a formal Swedish dinner or expecting to have to go to Stockholm to pick up his or her Nobel Prize:*

> Host usually starts by a toast of welcome.
>
> Host then usually drinks with the ladies, one at a time.
>
> Hostess usually begins by drinking with the gentlemen, one at a time.
>
> Guests *do not* toast host or hostess.
>
> Gentlemen toast the ladies, beginning with lady on right, then on left.
>
> Ladies usually do not return the toast.
>
> Gentlemen toast each other.
>
> The older or more prominent person always takes the initiative; the younger returns the toast before the end of dinner.
>
> Some younger ladies return older ladies' toasts, some don't.
>
> You usually answer a toast in the same wine.

After a Quarrel

Here's looking at you, though
heaven knows it's an effort.

Before an Exam

If we must suffer, let us suffer nobly.

—VICTOR HUGO

Cocktail Party

To the cocktail party: where olives are speared and friends stabbed.

Conscience, Moments of

Here's to a clear conscience—or a poor memory.

Here's to Conscience. May it waken to hear us toast it and
then go to sleep again.

Expectant Parents

Here's to one who born will be,
Born of the body, sowed of the soul,
Born of the flesh of you and me.

Out of a love our child will grow. . . .
Greater than light, deeper than dark,
All other love is but a spark.

Here is the toast of the moon and the stars,
To the child . . . who will soon be ours.

Four of Us

Here's to the four of us!
Thank God there's no more of us!
or
One bottle for four of us!
Thank God there's no more of us!

The Graduate

A *toast to the Graduate—in a class by him/herself.*

Imperfect Love

Here's to the man who can bravely say,
"I have loved her all my life—
Since I took her hand on the wedding day
I have only loved my wife!"
Would we not praise him long and well
With the strongest praise that is,
The man who could boldly, firmly tell,
And stick to—a lie like this?

Marriage is a lot like the army, everyone complains, but you'd be surprised at the large number that reenlist.

—*Actor* JAMES GARNER

'Tis better to have loved and lost,
Than to marry and be bossed.

You may prate of the virtue of memory,
   Of the days and joys that are past,
But here's to a good forgettery,
   And a friendship that cannot last!

You may talk of a woman's constancy,
   And the love that cannot die,
But here's a health to a woman's coquetry,
   And the pleasure of saying "Good-Bye"!

—*A written toast left at the Wayside Inn*
from Henry Wadsworth Longfellow's Tales
of a Wayside Inn.

Introductory

Here's mud in your eyes—while I look
Over your beautiful sweetheart!

Late Arrival

Here's to the Clock!
  Whose hands, we pray heaven,
When we come home at three,
  Have stopped at eleven!

—OLIVER HERFORD *and*
JOHN CECIL CLAY, *"Happy Days"*

I crept upstairs, my shoes in hand,
  Just as the night took wing,
And saw my wife, four steps above,
  Doing the same damned thing.

Then fill a fair and honest cup, and bear it straight to me;
The goblet hallows all it holds, what'er the liquid be;
And may the cherubs on its face protect me from the sin
That dooms one to those dreadful words,
  "My dear, where have you been?"

—OLIVER WENDELL HOLMES

Lying

The lie—an abomination unto the Lord, and a very present help in time of trouble.

Nightcap

In days of old the night-cap
Was worn outside the head:
Let's put ours in the inside.
And then—let's go to bed.

—W. E. P. FRENCH

May you sleep like a log, but not like a sawmill.

On the Road

Here's to you and here's to me,
Whenever we may roam;
And here's to the health and happiness
Of the ones who are left at home.

On the Trail

A health to the man on the trail tonight;
may his grub hold out; may his dogs keep their legs;
may his matches never misfire.

—JACK LONDON

Opening Night

A hit, a very palpable hit.

—SHAKESPEARE, Hamlet, *Act V*

Quiet Evening

To the Homely Three: A good book, a bright light, and an easy chair.

Religion

To Church: The first time one goes he has water thrown on him, the second time he has rice thrown on him, the third time he has dirt thrown on him.

Rioting, to the Prevention of

O'Bacchus who hath sent us wine,
Give us now, we pray,
Wit with drink.
And Thou, Minerva, wisdom send,
That we may abstain from rioting.

Rumors

Two ears and but a single tongue
    By nature's laws to man belong.
The lesson she would teach is clear,
    Repeat but half of what you hear.

Second Choice

Here's to you, my dear,
And to the dear that's not here, my dear;
But if the dear that's not here, my dear,
Were here, my dear,
I'd not be drinking to you, my dear.

Three of Us

I'm as dear to you as he,
He's as dear to me as thee,
You're as dear to him as me,
Here's to "Three's good company."

Trouble

Here's to ya,
Here's for ya,
I wish to hell
I never saw ya.

A Very Special Interlude

Where is the heart that would not give
Years of drowsy days and nights,
One little hour like this to live—
Full to the brim of life's delight?

—TOM MOORE

The Bachelor

Here's to single blessedness!

The Bad Singer

Swans sing before they die: 'twere no bad thing
Did certain persons die before they sing.

The Bore

Again I hear that creaking step—
He's rapping at the door!—
Too well I know that boding sound
That ushers in a bore.

I do not tremble when I meet
The stoutest of my foes,
But heaven defend me from the man
Who comes—but never goes.

Society is now one polished horde,
Formed of two mighty tribes—the bores and bored.

The Bore: May he give us a few brilliant flashes of silence.

The Cowboy

Here's to luck, and hoping God will take a likin' to us!

—*Cowboy, Dakota Territory, circa 1880*

Up to my lips and over my gums;
Look out guts, here she comes.

—*Cowboy toast collected by John and Alan*
Lomax for their Cowboy Songs and Other
Frontier Ballads (*1916 edition*)

Creditors

Here's to our creditors—may they be
Endowed with three virtues:
Faith, Hope, and Charity!

Here's to the creditor—
  Long may he waive.

Fat People

A toast to us, my good, fat friends,
To bless the things we eat;
For it has been full many a year,
Since we have seen our feet.

Yet who would lose a precious pound,
By trading sweets for sours?
It takes mighty girth indeed,
To hold such hearts as ours!

—WALLACE IRWIN, *"Fat Man's Toast,"* *1904*

The Financially Indisposed

'Tis easy enough to say: "Fill 'em!"
When your bank doesn't say: "Overdrawn."
  But the man worthwhile,
  Is the man who can smile,
When every darned cent is gone.

Fools

Let us toast the fools; but for them the rest of us could not
succeed.

—MARK TWAIN

The Gardener

From the earth we were formed,
　To the earth we return . . .
And in between we garden.

> —NELSON EDDY, *contributing writer to*
> A Gentleman's Guide to Toasting

May the weeds wilt before you; may the vegetables rise up to feed you; and may the bugs stay always on the other side of the fence.

> —*Quoted as an "old hoer's prayer" by*
> KATHRYN E. MASON *in* The American
> Way *magazine, December 1982*

The Hobo

To the holidays—all 365 of them.

The Liar

May every liar be blessed with a good memory!

> —MARK TWAIN

Member of Congress

May the members of Congress, while they are in Washington, never forget that they are the representatives of the people.

Misers

Here's to misers—whose abstinence gives us the more to drink.

Mothers-in-Law

Here's to our dear old mother-in-law,
  With all her freaks and capers,
For were it not for dear old ma,
  What would become of the "comic papers"?

Omar Khayyám

Here's to old Omar Khayyám—
  I'm stuck on that beggar—I am!
His women and wine are something divine—
  For his verses I don't care a damn!

Richard Wagner

Here's to you, Richard Wagner,
  With your horns and your bassoons;
What a hit you'd have made in music
  Had you only tackled tunes.

The Smoker

It isn't the cough
That carries you off;
It's the coffin
They carry you off in.

The Spender

Lift 'em high and drain 'em dry
To the guy who says, "My turn to buy!"

The Usurer

May you take as much interest in Heaven
As I know you have taken on Earth.

The Virgin

Here's to _____
For her, life held no terrors
Born a virgin, died a virgin
No hits, no runs, no errors.

SEE ALSO: *Professional and Occupational*

A drop of whiskey
Ain't a bad thing right here!

—BRET HARTE

A *Toast to the Three Great American Birds:*
   May you always have an Eagle in your pocket,
   A Turkey on your table,
   And Old Crow in your glass.

Don't die of love; in Heaven above
   Or hell, they'll not endure you;
Why look so glum when Doctor Rum
   Is waiting for to cure you?

—OLIVER HERFORD

Fifteen men on the Dead Man's Chest—
   Yo-ho-ho and a bottle of rum!
Drink and the devil had done for the rest—
   Yo-ho-ho and a bottle of rum!

—ROBERT LOUIS STEVENSON, Treasure Island

Here is to the Irish, a whiskey with heart,
that's smooth as a Leprechaun's touch,
yet as soft in its taste as a mother's embrace
and a gentleness saying as much.

Here's to the man without a shirt to his back,
May he deck himself out with a dickey;
And here's to the man, who of rums finds a lack,
May he fill himself up with gin rickey.

How beautiful the water is!
To me 'tis wondrous sweet—
For bathing purposes and such;
But liquor's better neat.

—MRS. C. O. SMITH

Keep your head cool and your feet warm,
And a glass of good whiskey will do you no harm.

On land or at sea
One need not be wary:
A well made old-fashioned
prevents *beri beri*

If wine tells truth, and so have said the wise;
It makes me laugh to think how brandy lies.

—OLIVER WENDELL HOLMES

Inspiring bold John Barleycorn,
What dangers thou cans't make us scorn
Wi' tippling we fear nae evil
Wi' usquebae [whiskey] we'll face the devil.

—ROBERT BURNS, *"Tam o'Shanter"*

Let those who will, praise fragrant wine,
That slowly brings on dizziness.
  Good whiskey, clear,
    To me is dear,
For two drinks does the business.

May we never be out of spirits.

No fluoride, No pollution. Just pure gin.

—*Caption to a Chon Day cartoon in*
Playboy *magazine*

Rum, rum, Jamaica rum,
Who in thy praise is dumb?
The rich, the poor, the gay, the glum,
All call thee good, Jamaica Rum.

—SIR ARTHUR SULLIVAN

This cordial julep here
That flames and dances in its crystal bounds.

—JOHN MILTON, Comus

Well, if it isn't gin,
Was meant to do us in,
The chances are it's lemonade or dates.

—A. P. HERBERT *in Peter Owen's* A
History of Gin

SEE ALSO: *Libations; Mornings After; Revelry*

*It would appear that people who write good toasts tend to fish and play
poker rather than, say, hunt and play tennis. As the following toasts seem
to illustrate, the great toasters have gotten their exercise from hoisting
glasses.*

A little whiskey now and then
Is relished by the best of men;
It surely drives away dull care,
And makes ace high look like two pair.

Camp life is just one canned thing after another.

—*Toast to camping*

Gentlemen, the Queen!
She gazed at us serene,
She filled his flush,
Amidst the hush—
And gathered in the green.

Not the laurel—but the race,
Not the quarry—but the chase;
Not the dice—but the play
May I, Lord, enjoy always!

Poker—Like a glass of beer, you draw to fill.

The hand that rocks the cradle
  Is the hand that rules the earth—
But the hand that holds four aces!
  Bet on it for all you're worth.

There was a man in our town,
  And he was wondrous wise.
He jumped into a tournament
  And came out with a prize.
And when he saw the cup he'd won,
  With all his might and main,
He jumped into ten entry lists
  But never won again.

They have carried the American name to the uttermost parts of the earth—and covered it with glory every time. That is a service to sentiment; but they did the general world a large practical service, also—a service to the great science of geography. . . . Why, when those boys started out you couldn't see the equator at all; you could walk right over it and never know it was there. . . . But that is all fixed now . . . and so I drink long life to the boys who ploughed a new equator round the globe stealing bases on their bellies!

—MARK TWAIN, *to the members of the*
returning Spalding Baseball Tour of the World, 1889

SEE ALSO: *Fishing*

temperant

A fig then for Burgundy, Claret or Mountain,
  A few scanty glasses must limit your wish.
But here's to the toper that goes to the fountain,
  The drinker that verily "drinks like a fish."

—THOMAS HOOD

Bacchus has drowned more men than Neptune.

Balm of my cares, sweet solace of my toils!
  Hail just benignant!
To the unknown beloved
  This is my good wishes.

—*Coffee toast*

Black as the devil,
Strong as death,
Sweet as love, and
Hot as hell!

—*Coffee toast*

Cold water: We never want cash to buy it, we are never
ashamed to ask for it, and never blush to drink it.

Drinking water neither makes a man sick, nor in debt, nor
his wife a widow.

He believes in drinking quantities of water
Undiluted by the essence of the grape.

—HARRY GRAHAM

Here's to wine—safer outside than in.

I have found water everywhere that I have traveled.

> —THOMAS COOK, *founder of the*
> *international tour company*

If you drink like a fish,
Drink what a fish drinks.

Lips that touch wine jelly
Will never touch mine, Nellie.

O' Water for me! Bright Water for me,
And wine for the tremulous debauchee.

> —McGuffey's New Eclectic Speaker, *1858*

Our drink shall be water, bring, sparkling with glee
The gift of our God, and the drink of the free.

There is a devil in every berry of the grape.

> —*The Koran*

Water—ever bracing, ever satisfying, ever plenty, and never
mocking.

SEE ALSO: *Historic*

. . .

214

toastmaster

Four toasts for the person who hardly ever gets toasted.

A toastmaster is a person who eats a meal he doesn't want so he can get up and tell a lot of stories he doesn't remember to people who've already heard them.

—GEORGE JESSEL

An ambidextrous man is he;
　Watch closely, and you'll understand,
A wonder in his way—you see,
　He can toastmast with either hand.

Every rose has its thorn,
　There's fuzz on all the peaches;
There never was a dinner yet
　Without some lengthy speeches.

To the person who goes around introducing people who need no introduction.

We'll bless our toastmaster,
Wherever he may roam,
If he'll only cut the speeches short
And let us all go home.

tongue twisters

Five traditional toasts that not only express a sentiment but double as sobriety tests.

Here's a health to all those that we love,
Here's a health to all those that love us,
Here's a health to all those that love them that love those
    that love them
that love those that love us.

Here's a health to you and yours who have done such things
for us and ours; and when we and ours have it in our powers
to do for you and yours what you and yours have done for us
and ours, then we and ours will do for you and yours what
you and yours have done for ours.

Here's to you two and to we two,
If you two love we two
As we two love you two
Then here's to we four!
But if you two don't love we two
As we two love you two,
Then here's to we two and no more.

Here's to you,
    Here's two to you,
And two to you two, too,
    And to you two, too, here's two.

· · ·

Tho' a kiss be a-miss,
She who misses the kisses
As Miss without kiss
May miss being a Mrs.
And he who, a-miss,
Thinks both Missed and Kisses
Will miss Miss and Kiss
And the kisses of Mrs.

Ultimate Toasts

The "ultimate" toast is that in which the toast is made, the drink drained at one gulp, and the glass thrown to the floor, against a wall, or into the fire. They were in style when the czars ruled Russia, during the days of George III in England when one toasted the king (as no lesser mortal was supposed to be honored from the same glass), and in the great banquet halls of seventeenth- and eighteenth-century Scotland. Commonly such toasts were proposed with all the participants placing their right foot on their chairs and their left foot on the table.

The traditional Scottish ultimate toast is made with these words:

Up with it, up with it, up with it!
Down it, down it, down it!
From me, from me, from me!
To me, to me, to me!
May all your days be good, my friend!
Take it down!
And no other shall drink from this glass again evermore!

At this point the glass was thrown with gusto over the left shoulder.

Ultimate toasts are now definitely out of style. A pity, because they could do a lot to liven up suburban dinner parties.

weddings

"Health and happiness" and "May all your troubles be little ones" are the most common wedding toasts. They have become cliché. Some options:

A Second Marriage: To the triumph of hope over experience.

—SAMUEL JOHNSON, *1770*

A toast to love and laughter and happily ever after.

A toast to the groom—and discretion to his bachelor friends.

Down the hatch, to a striking match!

Drink, my buddies, drink with discerning,
Wedlock's a lane where there is no turning;
Never was owl more blind than lover;
Drink and be merry, lads; and think it over.

—*Bachelor party toast*

Grow old with me!
The best is yet to be,
The last of life,
For which, the first is made.

—ROBERT BROWNING

Here's *to my* mother-in-law's daughter,
   Here's to *her* father-in-law's son;
And here's to the vows we've just taken,
   And the life we've just begun.

218

Here's to the bride and mother-in-law,
Here's to the groom and father-in law,
Here's to sister and brother-in-law,
Here's to friends and friends-in-law,
May none of them need an attorney-at-law.

Here's to thee and thy folks from me and my folks;
And if thee and they folks love me and my folks
As much as me and my folks love thee and thy folks,
Then there never was folks since folks was folks
Loved me and my folks as much as thee and thy folks.

Here's to the Bride and the Groom!
   May you have a happy honeymoon,
May you lead a happy life,
   May you have a bunch of money soon,
And live without all strife.

Here's to the bride that is to be,
   Here's to the groom she'll wed,
May all their troubles be light as bubbles
   Or the feathers that make up their bed!

Here's to the groom with bride so fair,
And here's to the bride with groom so rare!

Here's to the happy man: All the world loves a lover.

                                        —RALPH WALDO EMERSON

219

Here's to the husband—and here's to the wife;
May they remain lovers for life.

I drink to myself and one other,
And may that one other be he
Who drinks to himself and one other,
and may that one other be me.

It is written:
"When children find true love,
parents find true joy."
Here's to your joy and ours,
from this day forward
　　　—Parents' toast

Let us toast the health of the bride;
　Let us toast the health of the groom,
Let us toast the person that tied;
　Let us toast every guest in the room.

Look down you gods,
And on this couple drop a blessed crown.

　　　　　　　　　　　　　　—SHAKESPEARE

Love, be true to her; Life, be dear to her;
Health, stay close to her; Joy, draw near to her;
Fortune, find what you can do for her,
Search your treasure-house through and through for her,
Follow her footsteps the wide world over—
And keep her husband always her lover.

　　　　　　　　　　—ANNA LEWIS, *"To the Bride"*

Marriage: A community consisting of a master, a mistress,
and two slaves—making in all, two.

　　　　　　　　　　　　　—AMBROSE BIERCE

Marriage has teeth, and him bit very hot.

—*Jamaican proverb*

Marriage *is a wonderful institution, but who wants to live in an*
institution.

—GROUCHO MARX

May their joys be as bright as the morning, and their sorrows
but shadows that fade in the sunlight of love.

May their joys be as deep as the ocean
And their misfortunes as light as the foam.

May we all live to be present at their Golden Wedding.

May you grow old on one pillow.

—*Armenian*

May you have many children
and may they grow as mature in taste
and healthy in color
and as sought after
as the contents of this glass.

—*Irish*

May you live forever, may I never die.

May your love be as endless as your wedding rings.

May your wedding days be few and your anniversaries many.

May you have enough happiness to keep you sweet; enough trials to keep you strong; enough sorrow to keep you human; enough hope to keep you happy; enough failure to keep you humble; enough success to keep you eager; enough friends to give you comfort; enough faith and courage in yourself, your business, and your country to banish depression; enough wealth to meet your needs; enough determination to make each day a better day than yesterday.

Needles and pins, needles and pins
When a man marries his trouble begins.

Never above you. Never below you. Always beside you.
—WALTER WINCHELL

The greatest of all arts is the art of living together.
—WILLIAM LYON PHELPS

There is nothing nobler or more admirable than when two people who see eye to eye keep house as man and wife, confounding their enemies and delighting their friends.
—HOMER, Odyssey, *ninth century B.C.*

These two, now standing hand in hand,
    Remind us of our native land,
For when today they linked their fates,
    They entered the United States.

To my wife,
My bride and joy.

To the newlyweds: May "for better or worse" be far better than worse.

You don't marry one person; you marry three—the person you think they are, the person they are, and the person they are going to become as the result of being married to you.

—RICHARD NEEDHAM, You and All the
Rest, *edited by Jean Shagbaum
(M. Sutkiewicz, Toronto) quoted in*
Reader's Digest, *December 1983*

You only get married for the second time once.

—GARRISON KEILLOR, *quoted in* Forbes,
November 2, 1987

Wedlock's like wine—not properly judged of till the second glass.

—ERNEST JARROLD

SEE ALSO: *Anniversaries: Husbands; Wives*

A bottle of good wine, like a good act, shines ever in the retrospect.

—ROBERT LOUIS STEVENSON, *in "The
Silverado Squatters"*

A warm toast.
Good company.
A fine wine.
May you enjoy all three.

Any port in a storm.

Balm of my cares, sweet solace of my toils, Hail justice
benignant!

—THOMAS WHARTON

Clean glasses and old corks.

Comrades, pour the wine tonight
For the parting is with dawn;
Oh, the clink of cups together,
With the daylight coming on!

—RICHARD HOVEY

Count not the cups; not therein lies excess
In wine, but in the nature of the drinker.

Drink wine, and live here blitheful while ye may;
The morrow's life too late is,—live today!

For of all labors, none transcend
The works that on the brain depend;
Nor could we finish great designs
Without the power of generous wines.

Give of your wine to others,
   Take of their wine to you.
Toast to life, and be toasted awhile,
   That, and the cask is through.

—JAMES MONROE MCLEAN, The Book of Wine

God, in His goodness, sent the grapes
To cheer both great and small;
Little fools will drink too much,
And great fools none at all.

God made Man,
Frail as a Bubble
God made Love
Love made Trouble
God made the Vine
Was it a sin
That Man made Wine
To drown Trouble in?

—OLIVER HERFORD, The Deb's Dictionary

Good wine makes good blood;
Good blood causeth good humors;
Good humors cause good thoughts;
Good thoughts bring forth good works;
Good works carry a man to heaven.
Ergo:
Good wine carrieth a man to heaven.

—JAMES HOWELL, *to Lord Clifford early*
seventeenth century

He that drinks is immortal
For wine still supplies
What age wears away;
How can he be dust
That moistens his clay?

—H. PURCELL

225

He who clinks his cup with mine,
Adds a glory to the wine.

—GEORGE STERLING

Here's a bumper of wine; fill thine, fill mine:
Here's a health to old Noah, who planted the vine!

—R. H. BARHAM

Here's to mine and here's to thine!
  Now's the time to clink it!
Here's a flagon of old wine,
  And here we are to drink it.

—RICHARD HOVEY

Here's to old Adam's crystal ale,
Clear, sparkling and divine,
Fair H_2O, long may you flow,
We drink your health (in wine).

—OLIVER HERFORD

Here's to the man who knows enough
To know he's better without the stuff;
Himself without, the wine within,
So come, me hearties, let's begin.

Here's to the man
Who owns the land
That bears the grapes
That makes the wine
That tastes as good
As this does.

Here's to Water, water divine—
  It dews the grapes that give us wine.

I often wonder what the vintners buy
One half so precious as the stuff they sell.

—OMAR KHAYYÁM

Let those who drink not, but austerely dine, dry up in law;
the Muses smell of wine.

—HORACE

Then a smile, and a glass, and a toast and a cheer,
For all the good wine, and we've some of it here.

—OLIVER WENDELL HOLMES

This bottle's the sun of our table,
  His beams are rosy wine;
We, plants that are not able
  Without his help to shine.

This wine is full of gases
  Which are to me offensive,
It pleases all you asses
  Because it is expensive.

—A. P. HERBERT

To the big-bellied bottle.

When I die—the day be far!
Should the potters make a jar
Out of this poor clay of mine,
Let the jar be filled with wine!

When wine enlivens the heart
May friendship surround the table.

Wine and women—May we always have a taste for both.

Who was it, I pray,
  On the wedding day
Of the Galilean's daughter
  With a touch divine
  Turned in wine
Six buckets of *filtered* water?

—OLIVER WENDELL HOLMES

Wine improves with age—I like it more the older I get.

SEE ALSO: *Alliterative; Biblical; Celia's Toast; Champagne; General; Libations; Prohibition; Revelry*

A good wife and health
Are a man's best wealth.

Here's to the man who takes a wife,
Let him make no mistake:
For it makes a lot of difference
Whose wife it is you take.

To our wives and sweethearts. May they never meet!

Late last night I slew my wife,
Stretched her on the parquet flooring:
I was loath to take her life,
But I had to stop her snoring.

A health to our widows. If they ever marry again may they do
as well!

SEE ALSO: *Anniversaries; Weddings; Woman/Women*

Drink to fair woman, who, I think,
   Is most entitled to it;
For if anything drives men to drink,
   She certainly can do it.

Fill, fill, fill a brimming glass
Each man toast his favorite lass,
He who flinches is an ass,
Unworthy of love or wine.

Here's looking at you, dear!
Though I should pour a sea of wine,
My eyes would thirst for more.

Here's to God's first thought, "Man"!
Here's to God's second thought, "Woman"!
Second thoughts are always best,
So here's to Woman!

Here's to the gladness of her gladness when she's glad,
Here's to the sadness of her sadness when she's sad;
But the gladness of her gladness,
And the sadness of her sadness,
Are not in it with the madness of her madness when she's
mad.

Here's to the lasses we've loved, my lad,
Here's to the lips we've pressed;
   For of kisses and lasses,
Like liquor in glasses,
   The last is always the best.

I have never studied the art of paying compliments to
women, but I must say that if all that has been said by orators
and poets since the creation of the world in praise of women
were applied to the women of America, it would not do them
justice. God bless the women of America.

—ABRAHAM LINCOLN

Let her be clumsy, or let her be slim,
   Young or ancient, I care not a feather;
So fill up a bumper, nay, fill to the brim,
   Let us toast all the ladies together.

Of all your beauties, one by one,
   I pledge, dear, I am thinking;
Before the tale were well begun
   I had been dead of drinking.

They talk about a woman's sphere as though it had a limit;
There's not a place on earth or heaven,
There's not a task to mankind given,
There's not a blessing or a woe,
There's not a whispered yes or no,
There's not a life or birth,
That has a feather's weight of worth—
   Without a woman in it.

To the ladies, God bless them,
May nothing distress them.

To woman in her higher, nobler aspects, whether wife,
widow, grass widow, mother-in-law, hired girl, telegraph
operator, telephone helloer, queen, book agent, wet nurse,
stepmother, boss, professional fat woman, professional
double-headed woman, or professional beauty—God bless her.

—MARK TWAIN

'Tween woman and wine a man's lot is to smart,
For wine makes his head ache, and woman his heart.

We've toasted the mother and daugher
We've toasted the sweetheart and wife;
But somehow we missed her,
Our dear little sister—
The joy of another man's life.

What, sir, would the people of the earth be without woman? They
would be scarce, sir, almighty scarce.

—MARK TWAIN

SEE ALSO: *General; Love; Lust: Parents; Wives: Weddings*

world's
worst toasts

Over time, the human mind has composed a mind-numbing accumulation of bad toasts. Even the most seemingly narrow category of toast is liable to produce a set of genuine groaners. For instance, take the hardware business and try to decide which of these is the worst:

> To the hardware dealer: Who, if he keeps hammering away on the level, will nail plenty of customers, providing he's on the square. That's plane to see.
>
> *or*
>
> Here's to the fellow who can stand on his own two feet and face the world squarely without blinking an eye. He calls a spade a spade.
>
> *or*
>
> To the hardware trade—although they profess to honesty, they sell iron and steel for a living.

Here is a mercifully small selection of the author's all-star best of the worst.

A hobo is seen by the side of the road running a lighted match up and down the seams of his shirt by a passerby who asks, "What are you doing?" Hobo: "Toasting the visitors."

A pretzel and un stein o'peer,
And thou, mit sixteen kinder,
Ach, my lieber frau,
Sitting beside me, those garden in—
Ach! dat were baradise already now!

A wee little dog passed a wee little tree.
Said the wee little tree, "Won't you have one on me?"
"No" said the little dog, no bigger than a mouse. "I just had one on the house."

An amoeba named Joe and his brother
Went out drinking toasts to each other.
  In the midst of their quaffing
  They split their sides laughing
And found that each one was a mother.

Dismay to unskilled surgeons—who, like the nocturnal feline,
mew-till-late and destroy patients.

Here's to love, ain't life grand!
Just got a divorce from my old man.
I laughed and laughed at the judge's decision;
He gave him all the kids,
And none of 'em were his'n!

Here's to the Laplanders—cold and haughty: And here's to
their southern sisters—not quite so much so.

I *feel just like a loaf of bread. Wherever I go—they toast me.*

I propose a little toast.
You'll have to do better than that—I'm hungry.

Let us drink a toast to the queer old dean.

> *—Toast allegedly proposed by the Reverend*
> *William A. Spooner to Queen Victoria, his "dear*
> *old queen." Spooner, of course, was responsible*
> *for innumerable "tips of the slongue."*

May the village "belle" never be too long in the clapper!

> *—Old English*

May those who'd be rude to American roses
Feel a thorn's fatal prick in their lips and their noses.

· · ·

O Woman! Lovely Woman!
You're just like a gun;
You're loaded up with powder
And wadded most a ton
You set your cap with care,
And with a "bang" you slyly shoot
Your eyeballs at his stare. Oh Fudge!

To Hay Fever—here's looking at-choooo!

To *the one we love—when she is our toast we don't want any* but her.

We stand with the Philippines. We love your adherence to
democratic principles and democratic processes. We will not
leave you in isolation.

> —VICE PRESIDENT GEORGE BUSH,
> *representing the Reagan administration at*
> *the inauguration of Philippine President*
> *Ferdinand E. Marcos.* Reported in the
> Washington Post, *July 1, 1981.*

When the governor of the Virgin Islands was visiting
Washington, D.C., the toastmaster became flustered during his
introduction and announced, "It's a great pleasure to present
the Virgin of Governor's Island."

> —Teacher's Treasury of Stories for Every Occasion,
> *edited by M. Dale Baugham (Prentice-Hall)*
> quoted in Reader's Digest, *April 1985*

Woman's hair; beautiful hair,
  What words of praise I'd utter—
But, oh, how sick it makes me feel,
  To find it in the butter.

Acknowledgments

I break my bones before you.

—*Japanese. It refers to
the severest form of genuflection.*

The idea for my toast collection first came to me during the summer of 1977 after I had bought, for a nickel, a slim book of toasts at a library book sale in Maine. That collection, which was published in 1908, got me started as a compiler of toasts, and so my first indebtedness must go to Idelle Phelps, the author of *Your Health!*

Beyond Ms. Phelps a number of contemporary institutions and individuals have joined my conspiracy to revive the toast. First, I am obliged to a legion of reference librarians spread geographically from Boston to San Diego who helped me get a bead on my dusty quarry. The staffs of the Library of Congress, the Wayne State University Folklore Archives, the Tamony Collection of the University of Missouri, and the Public Library of Cincinnati and Hamilton County were extraordinarily helpful in this regard. Al Durante, a gentleman with A. Smith Bowman, the company that produces Virginia Gentleman, allowed me access to his fine collection of toasts for my original collection, as did the aforementioned gent from Dublin, Jack McGowan. Also thanks to Paul H. Emerson.

I would also like to thank a number of friends (John Masterman, Randy Roberts, Bob Skole, Joseph C. Goulden, Florenz Baron, Bob Snider, Elaine Viets, James Thorpe III, and Mariquita Mullan) for their contributions, not the least of which was their enthusiasm. Special thanks to Nelson Eddy to quote toasts by Jack Daniel, Tom T. Hall, Willard Scott, and Nelson Eddy from *A Gentleman's Guide to Toasting*. Bobbi Kadesch typed, corrected, and watched over the final manuscript. Neda Abrams of Guinness and M. K. Paskus, protocol officer at the U.S. Department of State, must also be singled out for their help. My mother, Isabelle C. Dickson, did her usual fine job as research assistant—in this case coming up with a dozen or so of the book's best toasts. Finally, thanks to Nancy to whom all the nice toasts under *Love* apply (to say nothing of a few under *Lust*).

Here's to all!

Bibliography

The cause of Bibliomania all over the world.

—Toast of the Roxburghe Club, 1812

More than three hundred sources were consulted for this collection; including many old books and booklets with the word toast *in the title. Here is a selected list of the most useful sources:*

Alderson, William, A. *Here's to You.* New York: Dodge Publishing Co., 1907.

Allen, Steve. *Curses or How Never to be Foiled Again.* Los Angeles: J. P. Tarcher, 1973.

Anderson, Will. *The Beer Book.* Princeton, N.J.: Pyne Press, 1973.

Antrim, Minna Thomas. *A Book of Toasts.* Philadelphia: Henry Altemus Co., 1902.

Aye, John. *Humor of Drinking.* London: Universal Publishing Co., 1934.

Benham, Sir Gurney. *Benham's Book of Quotations, Proverbs and Household Words.* New York: G. P. Putnam's, 1936.

Bennett, James O'Donnell. *When Good Fellows Get Together.* Chicago: The Reilly & Britton Co., 1908.

Berman, Frederick. *The Complete Toastmaster.* London: Blandford Press, 1953.

Birmingham, Frederick. *Falstaff's Complete Beer Book.* New York: Award Books, 1970.

Braude, Jacob. *Complete Speaker's and Toastmaster's Library.* 8 vols. Englewood Cliffs, N.J.: Prentice-Hall Inc., 1957.

Bibliography

Brooks, Fred Emerson. *Cream Toasts.* Chicago: Forbes and Co., 1915.

Butler, Anthony. *The Book of Blarney.* New York: Dell Publishing Co., 1969.

Case, Carleton B. *The Big Toast Book.* Chicago: Shrewsbury Publishing, 1927.

Chase, Edithe Lea, and Capt. W. E. P. French. *Waes Hael—The Book of Toasts.* New York: Grafton Press, 1904.

Clode, Edward J. *2088 Jokes, Toasts and Anecdotes.* New York: Grosset and Dunlap, 1921.

Cobb, Irvin S. *Irvin S. Cobb's Own Recipe Book.* Frankfort, Ky.: Frankfort Distilleries, 1934.

Connelly, Bertha, and Helen Ramsey. *Modern Toasts for All Occasions.* Minneapolis, Minn.: Northwestern Press, n.d.

Copeland, Lewis, and Faye Copeland. *10,000 Jokes Toasts and Stories.* Garden City, NY: Halcyon House, 1940.

Davis, Bert. *Crisp Toasts.* New York: H. M. Caldwell Co., 1907.

Dickson, Paul. *The Complete Book of the Best Toasts, Sentiments, Blessings, Curses and Graces.* New York: Delacorte Press, 1981.

Dodge, W. W. *The Fraternal and Modern Banquet Orator.* Burlington, Ia.: W. W. Dodge, 1903.

Dwiggins, Clare Victor. *Toast Book.* Philadelphia: John C. Winston Co., 1905.

Edmund, Peggy, and H. W. Williams. *Toaster's Handbook.* New York: H. W. Wilson & Co., 1914.

Einhorn, Benjamin. *Jewish Curses for All Occasions.* New York: Ace, 1970.

Eleven Cellars Wines. *A Book of Wine and Toasts.* Delano, Calif.: Eleven Cellars Wines, n.d.

Epsy, Willard R. *The Life and Works of Mr. Anonymous.* New York: Hawthorne Books, 1977.

Erdoes, Richard. *Saloons of the Old West.* New York: Knopf, 1979.

Fenno, R. F. *Toasts and Maxims.* New York: Fenno, 1908.

Fleming, Atheron. *Gourmet's Book of Food and Drink.* London: Bodley Head, 1933.

Fougner, G. Selmer. *Along the Wine Trail.* New York: The New York Sun Publishing Co., 1935.

French, Richard Valpy. *Nineteen Centuries of Drink in England.* London: Longmans, Green, and Co., 1884.

———. *The History of Toasting or Drinking of Healths in England.* London: National Temperance Publication Depot, n.d.

Friedman, Edward L. *Toastmaster's Treasury.* New York: Harper and Row, 1960.

Friedman, Gil. *A Dictionary of Love.* Arcata, Calif.: Yara Press, 1990.

Fuller, Edmund. *Thesaurus of Epigrams*. New York: Crown Publishers, 1943.

Fulmer, Dave. *A Gentleman's Guide to Toasting*, Oxmoor House for Jack Daniels Distillery, Lynchburg, Tenn.: 1990.

Garrison, Robert L. *Here's to You! 354 Toasts, You Can Use Today for Parties, Holidays, and Public Affairs*. New York: Crown, 1980.

Gayre, G. R. *Wassail! In Mazers of Mead*. London: Phillimore & Co., 1964.

Glover, Ellye Howell. *Dame Curtsey's Book of Novel Entertainments for Every Day of the Year*. Chicago: A. C. McClurg & Co., 1927.

Gray, Arthur. *Toasts and Tributes*. New York: Rhode & Haskins, 1904.

Hackwood, Frederick W. *Inns, Ales, and Drinking Customs of Old England*. London: T. Fisher Unwin, 1909.

Hartman, J. F. *Spice and Parody*. New York: The Outing Publishing Co., 1906.

Harvey, James Clarence. *Over the Nuts and Wine*. Boston: H. M. Caldwell, 1906.

Harwell, Richard Barksdale. *The Mint Julep*. Savannah: The Beehive Press, 1975.

Haverson, James P. *Sour Sonnets of a Sorehead*. Boston: H. M. Caldwell Co., 1908.

Henry, Lewis C. *Toasts for All Occasions*. Garden City, N.Y.: Halcyon House, 1949.

Herford, Oliver, and John Cecil Clay. *Happy Days*. New York: Mitchell Kennerley, 1917.

Hewitt, W. C. *The Best After-Dinner Stories and How to Tell Them*. Chicago: Charles T. Powner Co., 1946.

Hughes, T. *The Toastmaster's Guide*. London: Hughes, 1806.

Huston, Marvyn J. *Toasts to the Bride and How to Propose Them*. Rutland, Vt.: Charles Tuttle, 1968.

Iverson, William. *O the Times! O the Manners!* New York: William Morrow & Co., 1965.

Jeffery, Barbara. *Wedding Speeches and Toasts*. Slough, Berks, England: W. Foulsam & Co., Ltd., 1971.

Kaser, Arthur Leroy. *Good Toasts and Funny Stories*. Chicago: T. S. Denison & Co., Chicago, 1923.

Kearney, Paul W. *Toasts and Anecdotes*. New York: Edward J. Clode, 1923.

Koken, John M. *Here's to It!* New York: A. S. Barnes, 1960.

Lewis, E. C. *Toasts for All Occasions*. Boston: Mutual Book Co., 1903.

Lewis, E. L. *Everybody Up—A Book of Toasts*. Boston: H. M. Caldwell, 1909.

Loots, Barbara Kunz. *The Little Book of Toasts*. Kansas City: Hallmark, 1975.

Lowe, Paul E. *The 20th-Century Book of Toasts*. Philadelphia: David McKay, 1910.

McClure, John, and William Rose Benet. *The Stag's Hornbook*. New York: Knopf, 1945.

McCord, David. *What Cheer*. New York: Coward-McCann, 1945.

McIvor, Ivor Ben. *Scottish Toasts*. New York: H. M. Caldwell, 1908.

McLean, James Monroe. *The Book of Wine*. Philadelphia: Dorrance and Co., 1934.

Madison, Janet. *Toasts You Ought to Know*. Chicago: Reilly & Britton Co., 1908.

Marchant, W. T. *In Praise of Ale*. London: George Redway, 1888.

Morewood, Samuel. *Inventions and Customs of Ancient and Modern Nations in the Manufacture and Use of Inebriating Liquors*. Dublin, n.p. 1838.

Morrison, Lillian. *Yours Till Niagara Falls*. New York: Thomas Y. Crowell Co., 1950.

Muller, Helen M. *Still More Toasts*. New York: H. W. Wilson Co., 1932.

Murphy, J. F. *Five Hundred Popular and Up-To-Date Toasts*. Boston: J. F. Murphy, n.d.

Nesbit, Wilbur. *The Loving Cup: Original Toasts by Original Folks*. Chicago: P. F. Volland and Co., 1909.

Ott, Irv. *Popular Toasts*. Baltimore: Phoenix Publishing Co., 1904.

Owen, Peter. *A History of Gin*. London: 1976.

Phelps, Idelle. *Your Health!* Philadelphia: George W. Jacobs, 1906.

Prochnow, Herbert V. *Toastmaster's Handbook*. New York: Prentice-Hall, 1949.

Proskauer, Julien J. *What'll You Have?* New York: A. L. Burt, 1933,

Prynne, William. *Healthes: Sicknesse*. London: 1628.

Pudney, John. *The Harp Book of Toasts*. London: Harp Lager, 1963.

Ramsay, William. *A Book of Toasts*. New York: Dodge Publishing Co., 1906.

Reynolds, Cuyler. *The Banquet Book*. New York: G. P. Putnam, 1902.

Rice, Wallace, and Frances Rice. *Toasts and Tipple: A Book of Conviviality*. New York: M. A. Donohue and Co., 1914.

Roach, J. *The Royal Toastmaster*. London: Roach, 1791.

Rodgers, H. A. *Toasts and Cocktails*. St. Louis: Shallcross Printing and Stationary Co., 1905.

Rosten, Leo. *The Giant Book of Laughter*. New York: Bonanza, 1989.

Rowe, Col. William H., Jr. *Campaign Verse and Toasts*. Albany: J. B. Lyon and Co., 1908.

Schmidt, William. *The Flowing Bowl.* New York: Charles L. Webster, 1892.

"Shane Na Gael." *Irish Toasts.* New York: H. M. Caldwell, 1908.

Simon, Andrew Lewis. *Drink.* New York: Horizon Press, 1953.

Stafford, William Young. *Toasts and Speeches.* Chicago: Frederick J. Drake and Co., 1902.

Sullivan, James. *Smart Toasts for The Smart Set.* New York: M. J. Ivers, 1903.

Sutherland, Natalie M. *Toasts, Jokes and Limericks.* Reader Mail, 1937.

Toasts. St. Louis, Mo.: The William J. Lemp Brewing Co., 1896, 1908.

Viets, Elaine. "Here's Mud in Your Eye." St. Louis *Post-Dispatch,* December 26, 1976.

Waters, Margaret. *Toasts.* New York: Barse and Hopkins, 1909.

Williams, Victor W. *"Hello Bill" Toasts.* San Francisco: Whitaker & Ray Co., 1903.

Woolard, Sam F. *Good Fellowship.* Wichita, Kans.: Goldsmith Woolard Publishing Co., 1904.

Wright, Richardson. *The Bed-Book of Eating and Drinking.* Philadelphia: J. B. Lippincott, 1943.